Ocean Enough and Time

OCEAN ENOUGH AND TIME

Discovering the Waters Around Antarctica

James Gorman

HarperCollins*Publishers*

FIRST EDITION

Designed by Nancy Singer

Photograph insert designed by Maura Fadden Rosenthal

Library of Congress Cataloging-in-Publication Data

Gorman, James, 1949–
Ocean enough and time : discovering the waters around Antarctica / by James Gorman. — 1st ed.
p. cm.
Includes bibliographical references and index.
ISBN 0-06-016620-7
1. Antarctic Ocean. I. Title.
GC461.G68 1995
551.4689—dc20 94-23824

---

95 96 97 98 99 ❖/RRD 10 9 8 7 6 5 4 3 2 1

For Kate, Madeleine, Celia, and Daniel,
who nourish this inland soul,
on land and at sea.

Exultation is the going
Of an inland soul to sea
Past the houses—past the headlands—
Into deep Eternity—

Bred as we, among the mountains,
Can the sailor understand
The divine intoxication
Of the first league out from land?

Emily Dickinson

CONTENTS

Acknowledgments		xi
1	The Ocean	1
2	Breaking the Ice	17
3	Sealing	53
4	Port	75
5	Larval Shapes	93
6	Higher Forms	109
7	Whaling	125
8	Working the Water	143
9	The Ocean	159
Notes		171
A Note on Sources		179
Index		181

Photographs follow page 82.

ACKNOWLEDGMENTS

There are writers who work alone, but nobody gets to the Southern Ocean or the continent of Antarctica on his or her own. The number of people who helped me in my travels is great. First and foremost, I want to thank the National Science Foundation, which selected me to participate in its Artists and Writers Program and arranged my travel in the Southern Ocean and my chance to spend time at McMurdo Research Station. NSF personnel in Washington and Antarctica made my life as a reporter and writer as easy as it could be. Guy Guthridge, who runs this program for the NSF, is a good friend of writers, artists, scientists, and Antarctica itself. He did everything possible to enable me to go where I wanted and see what I wanted.

I traveled on the United States Coast Guard cutter *Polar Sea*, and I want to thank the officers and crew of the *Polar Sea* for their good spirits and helpfulness in putting up with a nosy landlubber. Particular thanks to Capt. Gary Boyer, Cmdr. Dale Thompson, Lt. Jorge Arroyo, Lt. Cmdr. Bill Shultz, Lt. Alda Siebrands, Lt. Ralph Hawes, and Lt. Cmdr. Wayne Roberts.

Among the scientists who helped me before, during, and after my trip, I want first of all to thank Stanley S. Jacobs of Lamont Doherty Earth Observatory, who pointed me in the right direction before my trip and after it undertook the thankless task of reading my manuscript in rough form. He made extremely helpful corrections and suggestions, but he is not, of course, responsible for any errors that may persist. Those are entirely my fault.

During my trip, Willie Weeks and Martin Jeffries were enormously helpful and generous with their time, as was Chuck Stearns, who let me hitchhike on trips by helicopter, Twin Otter, and Sprite. Jonathan Berg, a geologist whose work does not figure in this book, also generously enlisted me for a helicopter trip to Franklin Island.

All of the scientists and other people I mention in the book deserve thanks for their cooperation. I should thank again Donal Manahan, John Welborn, Larry Basch, and Jim Herpolsheimer. And thanks to the U.S. Navy helicopter pilots, the civilians in Antarctic Support Associates, and all of the support staff at McMurdo.

The work of the book was not all done in the Antarctic. The staff of the Mystic Seaport library in Mystic, Connecticut, were very helpful in my pursuit of material on sealing and whaling in Antarctic waters. And, for help in many ways both small and large, thanks to my patient and protective agent, Kris Dahl. Thanks to Rick Kot at HarperCollins for getting the project going and to Eamon Dolan for his forbearance and intelligence in helping to bring it to completion. Thanks also to Eleanor Mikucki, who provided attentive and sensitive copy editing.

Thanks to my friend and unofficial editor Richard Liebmann-Smith, who offered valuable suggestions at several points along the way. And most of all thanks to my family, to whom this book is dedicated. No book is easy to write, but this was a particularly difficult one for me to master. Writers' families probably suffer more during rough patches than writers themselves. I wish the completion of the book could bring them some particular reward for their patience and love, but the most I can offer is my deep gratitude.

Chapter 1

THE OCEAN

Roald Amundsen prepared for his south polar voyage by skiing on the Greenland ice cap and buying hardy Eskimo dogs. I prepared for mine by reading nature poetry and laying in a supply of antacids.

Amundsen was a man of action, headed for the South Pole and his vision of heroism—although he didn't mention his destination to anybody when he left. He needed to know how to ski. He needed those dogs. I was a man of introspection, shaped on the antiheroic last, the sort who favored gallows humor even though there was no gallows in sight, a traveler prey to gloom and dyspepsia in the best of circumstances. I needed those antacids.

I needed that poetry both as a spiritual antidote to knee-jerk nihilism and because I wanted to learn how to think about the natural world. Above all I hoped to see how others distinguished between the internal and external voyage, between the imagination and the event. As I prowled through collections of nature writing, essays, and poetry I came on a piece by Joyce Carol Oates called "Against Nature." In it she quotes Wallace Stevens: "In the presence of extraordinary actuality, consciousness takes the place of imagination."[1] As Oates points out, the sheer weight of nature's presence is both the attraction and the obstacle. For anyone addicted to the pleasures of the imagination, in thrall to the constant internal chatter of rumination and interpretation, nature, as commonly conceived, offers relief and adventure or, conversely, annihilation. How to see clearly what is outside? How to step back and find the curve of one's own lens and assess what distortions it produces? Can you—could I—find the shifting boundaries between the mountain out there and the mountain inside? Or, in this case, the sea?

I had been to the Antarctic once before, a trip that inspired this second, more ambitious effort. On my first trip I was often miserable, sick both with something the ship's physician called bronchopneumonia and with what Oates diagnosed as the writer's resistance to nature. I was swallowing tetracycline, not drinking the fine Chilean wines, resenting the fun everyone else was having, and indulging in a perverse denial of the power of the sea and the ice. Of course there was the inescapable influence of the physical experience, which colored my thoughts about the Antarctic in the most direct and unsubtle fashion. When you have chills and fever and want most of all to be in a warm bed with a down coverlet over you and a loved one wiping your brow, it is hard to appreciate the peculiar grandeur of ice, the minimalist appeal of desolate landscapes.

The purpose of that first trip was penguin-watching. I was to do a book on penguins. In the first conversation with my publisher I had assured her that it was inconceivable to write about the birds without seeing them in the wild. To my amazement she and my editor nodded assent and funded most of a three-week trip to Antarctica, South Georgia, and the Falkland Islands.

The trip started with a flight to Santiago, Chile, and continued by plane down to Puerto Williams, the southernmost town in the country. From there we embarked on a luxurious, German-staffed cruise ship, the *World Discoverer.* This particular cruise line was known for its amenities, including the cuisine, one example of which was pork cooked a delicate pink with a subtle green sauce. I remember reflecting on how far I had come in the world when this dish was served. My mother, who takes it as religious doctrine that beef should be served bloody and pork cooked until it crumbles, would have demanded a tribunal under the international law of the sea if she had been served pink pork on a cruise, whatever color the sauce.

The ship had two restaurants, two bars, and a swimming pool on the stern. The pool was empty on this trip, but one day at about 65 degrees south latitude and 50 degrees Fahrenheit we did gather around it to have a barbecue, a suburban ritual made slightly absurd by the presence of icebergs off port and starboard. We also had a meal one night catered by the ship's crew in an abandoned whalers' mess in the crumbling ghost town of Strom Ness on South Georgia, 1,000 miles east of Cape Horn. I believe the proper term for this kind of event is "piss elegant." In a tumbledown dining room where the working wretches of the whaling industry had downed their rations in squalor, we celebrated our position at the top of both the food chain and the socioeconomic ladder.

As cranky and contrary as I felt during that first trip, I began laying plans to go back almost as soon as the ship passed Cape Horn on its way to Antarctica. Back home, after the trip was over, friends would ask me if I had loved it—the Antarctic. Not exactly, I would say, trying to tell the truth without poor-mouthing my extraordinary good luck. I found it grim and harsh, I said. It seemed to me a good place to learn how inconsiderate Nature is of human beings. It's a common conceit of modern nature lovers that the world apart from humankind is somehow as beneficent as it was once considered malevolent. It seemed quite clear in the Antarctic that nature is thoroughly and completely indifferent.

That may, in fact, be the point of traveling to places of overwhelming grandeur—the bliss of being ignored. In the presence of cold immensity a traveler can't help but feel finally, blessedly, insignificant, and thus relieved of a host of worries. On this first trip, it was the ocean even more than the icy continent that seemed most immense, most indifferent. And it was the ocean to which I wanted to return.

Birds were what led me to think the ocean was approachable in a way the ice was not. I spent most of my time at sea watching birds, the names of most of which I did not know. There were numerous ecstatic moments when hosts of birds flew in front of my binoculars and I wanted to burst forth, like the first man in John Hollander's poem "Adam's Task," in a paroxysm of naming: "Thou, verdle; thou, McFleery's pomma; / Thou; thou; thou—three types of grawl."[2]

During a part of the voyage that took us from Elephant Island north and east of the Antarctic peninsula to South Georgia, we spent several days at sea. We had left the Antarctic continent and its offshore islands and were in the middle of the Southern Ocean. I had never been at sea before this trip, not out hundreds and hundreds of miles from land. The ocean was a puzzle. It was neither lush nor beautiful in an obvious way. It was vast, certainly, gray waves rolling to the horizon, prompting a shiver of awe. But after a short time it seemed to make most people sick or produce in them a tremendous desire to play bridge and read bad novels.

I wanted to keep looking at the ocean, but the opacity of the surface to both light and understanding made it difficult to pay it any sustained attention. There are landscapes and seascapes that are welcoming and lush, easy to savor—the Hudson River valley where I live, a coral reef. But not the open waters of cold seas. They resist and repel the casual visitor. They must be worked, in some way, in order to be known. Sailors learn to read the sea—its winds and currents. Fishermen learn the ocean bottom and the habits of fish. Scientists tow their instruments and their dredges, poring over the creatures they haul out of the water and the temperature gradients they record. And the kind of work you do defines the kind of ocean you see and understand.

On this cruise there were no working fishermen or scientists. The paying passengers who worked were another writer and I, a professional photographer or two, and a large contingent of bird-watchers. Almost half of the people on the cruise were birders. They were, most of them, a bit fanatical. In some, the obsession was a joyful one, in others, not. The birders did not seem to be on a frivolous vacation. They had paid $10,000 and up to take three weeks at the bottom of the world to glimpse certain seabirds with their Zeiss binoculars ($895 a pair, discount, at the time; I bought a pair for my next trip).

There were petrels and penguins, fulmars and albatrosses that the birders wanted to add to their life lists, and they would stand on the stern or bow, or sit in the observation lounge for hours at a time, their binoculars trained on the water. When news of a new bird came over the public address system they would charge up and down the ship's corridors, amusing some of the nonbirders, alienating others. During one of the elegant meals served onboard the birders would leap up, leave their wine in mid-sip, and dash to the window or the deck to record the sighting of a new bird.

In the midst of conspicuous luxury this kind of dedication was delightfully contrary. Some of these people seemed almost haunted by the possibility of missing a bird. In the midst of a landscape and seascape that reminded one of one's own insignificance, it was a quirky testament to human energy that anyone could turn bitter over having missed a bird for his life list.

In one incident there were some missed cues on an emperor penguin swimming by the ship, and just a few of the group got to see it. The voyage was only skirting emperor penguin territory, and there would be at most one or two fleeting opportunities to see one of these birds. If you missed your chance, the only thing to do would be to repeat the trip. After the botched emperor sighting, discontent spread among the disappointed like avian tuberculosis through a captive penguin colony. Those who had missed seeing it turned sullen and snappish, wine or no wine.

I spent a lot of time with the birders in the enclosed observation deck, watching through my own binoculars, staring at the sea until my eyes hurt and my arms cramped. Bird-watching was a way of working the ocean. The longer you stared, hunting birds, the more you forced the seascape to yield detail and complexity. Great wandering albatrosses flew by. Rafts of smaller black-browed albatrosses appeared on the water. Whale birds dived and whirled in the air around the boat. Pure white snow petrels flew around icebergs, visible only when seen against the background of the dark sea.

One afternoon, during the Elephant Island–South Georgia transit, as I scanned the sea left and right, looking for the dip and flash of wings, something new happened. Something bigger than a bird. In my view two minke whales breached; small whales, but whales nonetheless. (They take their name from a harpooner named Meincke who mistook one of these whales for a giant blue whale and shot. He was immortalized for his mistake. A blue whale can grow as long as 100 feet and a minke whale not more than 30.) They leaped and rolled, disappeared, blew, and breached again. I was overjoyed. The sight of whales leaping transforms the surface of the ocean as nothing else can, like a cry of joy during a commencement address. This performance lasted a few minutes, spray flying, whales rising and falling, rising and falling. By the time the public address system alerted all the ship's passengers, by the time the sluggardly novel readers got on deck to look, the whales were gone.

Even if they had arrived in time, as I did once or twice by rushing up from my cabin where I was sleeping or reading, they would not have shared the electric pleasure that I had drawn from the sighting. A whale spotted by someone else is not the same as a whale that bursts out of plain water before your eyes. Someone else's whale is just a whale, impressive but discrete, unconnected, out there. Your own whale is earned. It appears in the framework of time spent, of undisturbed water, of dues paid. It bursts out of the gray, rolling sameness like a prize, like land on the horizon. The surface of the water is all suggestion and mystery. The breaching of a whale is revelation. Eureka! you want to shout, or Leviathan! Or, like the lookout in an old song, "there's a whale, there's a whale, there's a whale fish, he cried, and she blows at every span."[3] Without the whale, the ocean is all promises. One can't help but feel, after hours or days without the appearance of any wonders, disappointed and skeptical. The whale delivers on the promise.

The Southern Ocean, whose surface my whale broke, is the world's only circumpolar ocean. It is a vast belt of fertile water around the cold, barren ice sheet of the continent, an ice sheet so enormous that it deforms the shape of the earth with its weight. At the earth's other pole, the Arctic Ocean is an ice-bound sea surrounded by land. At this pole, it is the sea that surrounds an ice-bound continent.

The biologist Sanford Moss writes of Antarctica: "It is the coldest, the driest, the windiest, the iciest, and (with its ice cap) averages as the highest in altitude of all the major land masses of our world. It has the least soil, the most fresh water, albeit in the form of ice, and it is surrounded by the stormiest ocean on earth."[4] The first to call this body of water the Southern Ocean was Captain James Cook. He saw a commonality in climate, winds, currents, and sea life all around the Antarctic. Today the Antarctic Circumpolar Ocean is another name for this polar sea. This term refers to the ocean south of the Polar Front (also called the Antarctic Convergence), the point at which cold, but fresher and therefore lighter, surface water moving northward from the continent starts to sink and mix with warmer water. In the space of a few miles, the surface temperature jumps several degrees, the sorts of microorganisms and krill in the water change, and there are often fogs and flocks of seabirds. The convergence is a shifting boundary; it moves and is farther north in some places than others. But since it was first observed its average latitude of 50 degrees south has been fairly stable.

The Southern Ocean is bigger than this circumscribed sea. It has no clearly defined northern boundary and sneaks up into the southern reaches of the Atlantic, Pacific, and Indian oceans, depending on who is using the term. I use "Southern Ocean" primarily to mean the Antarctic Ocean, the framework used for many scientific descriptions, but in looking at the history of exploration and sealing and whaling in these waters, I take a more liberal view, extending my consideration on occasion as far north as the passage around Cape Horn or the Cape of Good Hope.

Taking only the area south of the Antarctic Convergence, the Southern Ocean amounts to 10 percent of the world ocean, 36 million square kilometers. It unifies the other oceans. Like the United States, but more literally, it is a mixing bowl and a melting pot. The Atlantic, the Pacific, and the Indian oceans all feed warm water into it, and from the Antarctic continent comes cold fresh water from melting ice.

The ocean we see now, and its relation to the continents that fringe it and the one that it surrounds, is about 30 million years old. It began to form about 160 million years ago when the supercontinent Gondwanaland initially split apart. After 35 million years South America and Africa were separating and the Antarctic peninsula was still connected to South America. Fifty-three million years ago Australia split apart from East Antarctica, and from 38 to 29 million years ago the Antarctic continent moved south. The Drake Passage between South America and Antarctica grew. The west wind drift, or circumpolar current, came into being, helping to isolate Antarctica and allowing the deep freeze to begin.

The current ice cap dates from the end of that period. To put these dates in perspective, the earliest known penguin fossils are about 55 million years old. Penguins predate by millions of years the Antarctica of ice and snow, and the species that live there now are colonizers that have evolved to match the climate.

The Southern Ocean has its gyres and inconsistencies of wind and current, but on a grand scale it is steady. Around the Antarctic continent flows the circumpolar, eastward-moving current. Each second this current carries 130 million metric tons of water, more than twice the comparable freight of the Gulf Stream. Winds from the west accompany the current, and together they are called the West Wind Drift.

One surpassingly odd result of this prevailing current is recounted in the story of a famous open boat journey by the Antarctic explorer Ernest Shackleton. It is in fact one of the two most famous open boat journeys in the world. The other was by Captain Bligh after he was set adrift by the *Bounty* mutineers. (Bligh also had his Antarctic, Southern Ocean connection. He sailed with Captain James Cook when he circumnavigated Antarctica in the 1770s.) Bligh's voyage after the mutiny was in temperate seas. Shackleton's was in Antarctic waters, from Elephant Island in the South Orkneys to South Georgia. When he landed there, a thousand miles northeast of Cape Horn, he found a ships' graveyard, acres of shattered timber, bits of cargo, flotsam and jetsam. The wreckage was not from ships that foundered off South Georgia. It was from ships lost off Cape Horn. Their remnants had been carried a thousand miles by the West Wind Drift and had washed up on this shore.[5]

In the summer the ocean is open—only 4 million square kilometers are iced over—and the shores of its islands are covered with birds and seals in the millions. Penguins, albatrosses, and petrels nest on rocky shores and cliffs or burrow into the turf of the more northerly islands. Fur seals, sea lions, and elephant seals establish their rookeries. Once the whales were so numerous that explorers described the sea as alive and rippling with them.

Paradoxically, the life of the ocean is most often seen on land—at least by us surface creatures. The ocean, for all its richness, can seem as austere and harsh as the interior of the Antarctic continent. But on landfall at a seabird colony the noise and smell of mating birds in the millions, the barking and hollering of seals, the appalling stench and belching of sea elephants—all of this rolls over the traveler in waves of sound and odor. The transition from sea to shore is like that from a Buddhist temple to a bazaar.

Also paradoxically, it is the cold, lifeless continent that makes the sea rich. Meltwater from glaciers and ice shelves constantly replenishes the ocean, flowing outward from Antarctica in a surface current. The cold atmosphere of the continent also cools the surface ocean water, and freezing sea ice increases its salinity. Salty and cold, it is heavy enough to flow down through the surface and middle waters of the ocean to the bottom. This happens both near the continent and at the Polar Front. As the water sinks, deep water, rich with nutrients, wells up to replace it. The circulation of the ocean waters and the constant replenishing of the surface with nutrients are what feed the algae and plankton, which in turn feed shrimplike krill, which feed everything else.

In winter the pack ice spreads outward from the continent, and year-round icebergs and bergy bits make navigation hazardous. In "The Rime of the Ancient Mariner" the mariner's ship is blown south by a storm through fog and ice in the more southerly reaches of the Southern Ocean. Coleridge makes vivid in his poetry the details he gleaned from accounts of early polar voyages. "And now there came both mist and snow, / And it grew wondrous cold: / And ice, mast-high, came floating by, / As green as emerald."

Ice covers 20 million square kilometers of the Southern

Ocean in winter, 57 percent of its surface. This is sea ice, not the frozen freshwater ice shelves that ring the continent year round. These shelves, which are really the achingly slow outflow of the continental ice sheet, average a thickness of 450 meters. The biggest chunks of this freshwater ice—the Ross Ice Shelf in the Ross Sea below New Zealand and the Filchner-Ronne Shelf in the Weddell Sea, southeast of South America—account for two-thirds of the whole of Antarctica's ice shelves.

Though it has its intricacies, not least of which is the web of life at the ice edge where it meets the sea, the Southern Ocean is not a tremendously complex ecosystem like a tropical rain forest, with countless varieties of plants and animals linked in complex, crisscrossing patterns of competition and predation. The Southern Ocean is essentially simple, with relatively few species in very large numbers. Everything that lives in the Southern Ocean lives in abundance, or did once. And still the ocean can seem empty. For example, during their breeding seasons, penguins crowd nesting sites along the shores of Antarctica and the oceanic islands. But once breeding and raising chicks is finished, some of these penguins, such as the macaroni and rock hopper penguins, disappear at sea for up to six months. Nobody knows where they go. Each winter the Southern Ocean swallows tens of millions of penguins at a gulp, and each spring, like a penguin feeding its young with regurgitated fish, the ocean spills the birds out again on shore to squawk and fight and breed.

It is an ocean rich in history as well as natural history. Europeans first sailed south of Africa and South America in the late fifteenth and sixteenth centuries. Bartholomeu Dias and Vasco da Gama rounded the Cape of Good Hope in 1488 and 1497 respectively. Magellan found his straits in 1520. And from the 1770s, when Captain James Cook circumnavigated the Southern Ocean, charting its waters and reporting on its winds, its weather, its ice, its seals and whales, the ocean became a great sea road for commercial sailing vessels rounding the horn of South America and the tip of Africa, a bloody killing ground for sealers and whalers, a source of wealth and legendary stories, and a route to the Antarctic continent.

There is little record of exploration in the southern latitudes by aboriginal inhabitants of South America, New Zealand, or Australia. There is one bit of evidence that suggests some Pacific Islanders did once sail far enough south to run into icebergs. And some lance points found on the South Shetland Islands have encouraged speculation that Indians from Tierra del Fuego may have reached there.[6]

But it was when Europeans began sailing the Southern Hemisphere that the ocean was first charted. Amsterdam Island, south of the Indian Ocean, was first described in 1696, and then again in 1794. In one description the island was "so covered with wood rushes and thick canes entangled together, that one could not, in a day, go four miles." Sighted in 1788 by the H.M.S. *Bounty*, nearby St. Paul Island was described by the inestimable Captain Bligh as "verdant green."[7] Today, whether as the result of sealing and whaling, or some more natural process, those islands are bare and forbidding.

In general the islands of the Southern Ocean were considered hellish places. Kerguelen, south of the Indian Ocean, was called by New England sealers Desolation Island. Captain Cook thought South Georgia worthless. The inhabitants of far southern South America fared little better in the estimation of Europeans. Charles Darwin described the Fuegians as barely human:

> These poor wretches were stunted in their growth, their hideous faces bedaubed with white paint, their skins filthy and greasy, their hair entangled, their voices discordant, and their gestures violent. Viewing such men, one can hardly make oneself believe that they are fellow-creatures, and inhabitants of the same world.[8]

In the nineteenth century, the main harvest of the Southern Ocean consisted of fur seals killed for their pelts, which were taken dried to China and sold there to be made into fur felt for hats and other garments. The proceeds from the sale of pelts were invested in the goods of China, to be sold in Europe or at home in the United States. The first ship to come back from China with teas and fabrics, *Empress*, made 25 percent on investment for its backers.[9] Seal colonies were demolished on one island after another, to recover and be demolished again.

Whaling started in earnest in 1904, with motorized whale catchers and harpoon guns. The Southern Hemisphere is estimated to have held four times as many baleen whales as the Northern Hemisphere. And the Southern Ocean once supported about 1.1 million whales, with an estimated biomass of 45 million tons. By 1973 the numbers were down to half a million, but the figures for the biomass show a more startling decline, to 9 million tons. The bigger whales were harvested most heavily.[10]

It was this ocean I wanted to return to, and this ocean I wondered about. What was it to the sealers and whalers, to the scientists who study it, to the tourists? It was far too big to swallow in one metaphorical gulp, to define through one trip in one book. But it seemed that it might be possible to take sips—geographical, historical, scientific—and that the sips might add up to some sense of what the Southern Ocean has been and is. I wondered also what this cold sea would be to me. I was not an adventurer who could sail single-handed through the icebergs, or re-create Cook's voyages. Was there an expedition that would take me through the ocean, let me somehow come away with my own understanding of it?

When I was on the penguin cruise, I thought that if I had been able to pick my voyage to the Antarctic, to travel with whomever I wanted, to travel in time, my choice would not have been any of the famous Antarctic explorers like Scott, or Amundsen, or Shackleton, but a sealing captain out of a Connecticut port, New London or Stonington, say, in the early 1820s, when the sealers were denuding the South Shetland Islands of fur seals and discovering the continent of Antarctica. Somehow the raw greed and struggles of those voyages seemed more authentic to me than the expeditions of gentleman adventurers. I could not make that trip, of course, but I did promise myself that on my next trip I was not going to travel with tourists, but with some group that was working the water—like scientists.

They would have, if not the need and lust for wealth of the sealers, at least a healthy hunger for information and understanding. They would be grappling with the ocean in very particular terms, not simply floating on it, or gazing at it. They were bound to have a different relation to the water than I had developed on my first trip, voyaging as a pampered visitor.

I applied to the National Science Foundation, which has a program for artists and writers who want to visit the Antarctic. There are other ways to get to Antarctica—Greenpeace no longer has a presence there, but used to take on journalists. Adventure travel companies offer a variety of trips, ranging from vacations to severely challenging expeditions to the South Pole itself. One might even try to hitchhike on a Japanese "scientific" whaling voyage. But by far the biggest presence in Antarctica, with the most planes, boats, and bulldozers, is the U.S. Antarctic Program, run by the NSF. Three thousand people a season pass through the McMurdo Research Station on Ross Island.

I was accepted in the program and offered a trip on a U.S. Coast Guard icebreaker from Australia to Antarctica and back, a three-month trip, a chance to see a part of Antarctica I had not been to before and to spend time at sea, watch scientists at work, and go to ice-bound areas of the Southern Ocean hardly ever visited. I filled out all the forms, had my physical, and got a full set of dental X rays—the navy, which participates in the managing of the U.S. Antarctic Program, insists all needed dental work be completed before going to the ice. My passage through the bureaucracy left me duly accepted, vetted, examined, recorded, approved, and improved (the dental work).

A week or so before Christmas 1990, I left hearth, home, pregnant wife (second trimester), and two daughters and made the first leg of a three-month journey, a flight to Hobart, Tasmania, the southernmost part of Australia. From there I sailed for Antarctica on December 19 onboard the United States Coast Guard cutter *Polar Sea.*

Chapter 2

BREAKING THE ICE

Tasmania lies just south of the Australian mainland, with a main island of 26,000 square miles—about the size of Ireland—and a population of 500,000. Its climate is temperate. The air in Hobart, Tasmania, in December, the beginning of summer, is cool, about 50 degrees in the morning. And people seem as friendly and easygoing as those in any midwestern town.

It is a fitting jumping-off place for a voyage in the most remote of the world oceans since it is a kind of last outpost of empire, one of the last spots settled during the European expansion west and south. And it was settled with a vengeance. Within one hundred years of the first transported convicts arriving on the island as settlers, the Tasmanian aborigines, more technologically primitive than the mainland aborigines, had been virtually exterminated. They seem not to have been able to start a fire from scratch and carried hot coals or firebrands with them. They had no boomerangs, no nets, no dogs, no bone tools, and far more elementary stone tools than the people living on the mainland.[1]

The English colonizers set about exterminating the aborigines with a fury, shooting them, hunting them on horseback, torturing them, branding them. Sealers killed the men and kept the women, sometimes several for each man. In the 1800s bounties were set on them. The last recognized Tasmanian—her name was Truganini—died in 1876. Officially there are no aborigines left in Tasmania, although there are living descendants of European sealers and Tasmanian women.

I flew in from Sydney and spent several days exploring Hobart and the surrounding area, including a drive through sheep country to one of the original Australian penal colonies. I saw the spectacular coastline—rough, rocky palisades looking south on the Tasman Sea—a slow-moving echidna (one of only two living species of egg-laying mammals; the duck-billed platypus is the other), and flocks of wild parrots.

On my way back to Hobart after a hike I stopped in a small roadside inn called the Dunalley Hotel for lunch of fish chowder and tiger prawn salad with Australian beer, and listened to the men at the bar discuss the aborigines.

"I prefer to call them darkies."

"Black bastards."

"Every living thing has a place. Theirs just hasn't been dug yet."

"The abos have one big problem."

"What's that?"

"Breathing."

I felt a touch less nostalgic about leaving civilization after lunch.

My ship, my home for the next three months, was one of the two biggest conventionally powered icebreakers in the world. Sitting at the dock in Hobart, red with a white stripe on its bow, the *Polar Sea* exuded power and security. The *Polar Sea* is

400 feet long. It weighs 13,000 tons and is powered by six diesel engines and three gas turbines. The ship carries 1.3 million gallons of fuel and develops up to 75,000 horsepower. It was designed to travel at a maximum of 17 knots in open water, and to "ram its way through ice up to 21 feet thick and to steam continuously through ice 6 feet thick at a speed of three knots,"[2] an idealized projection, somewhat at variance with the ship's usual performance.

Like all icebreakers it has a rounded hull with no keel so that it will ride up on ice and sink through, using its weight to break a path. As a consequence of this shape, icebreakers are uncomfortable in rough weather; they behave something like a football in a bathtub. The *Polar Sea*'s maximum roll is 90 degrees. If it were to roll that far, the bridge, which is almost the width of the ship—a little more than 80 feet—would tilt until it was vertical. The penalty for not paying attention on the bridge in bad weather could be a broken rib, or arm, or worse. Indeed, a man had been killed on the *Polar Sea*'s bridge during rough weather.

I was joining the *Polar Sea* well into its yearly tour. It had left its home port of Seattle in October. From there it had motored south to Australia, stopping in Fiji for liberty. Just after leaving Seattle it had encountered rough weather. Everyone onboard, not just the numerous green crew members, had gotten sick. On the trip from Sidney to Hobart through the Tasman Sea the ship had encountered more heavy seas, doing 40-degree rolls. No one onboard the ship when I embarked had seen it roll more than 50 degrees on any cruise. And when it did roll, they said, its rolls were slow and even. In other words, though it might tip, it would almost certainly not tip over. In rough weather an icebreaker was uncomfortable, but safe.

On the day before we set sail, Christmas presents arrived. Or at least that's how I looked on the duffels of cold weather gear provided by the NSF. I have always been powerfully attracted to gear. I believe that this was a secret motivation for Amundsen also, and that lack of sufficient hunger for the neatest gear is one of the things that did in Robert Falcon Scott. Amundsen spent an enormous amount of time devising the appropriate boots and ski bindings, acquired or imitated Eskimo clothes, got the best dogs. Scott often sent somebody else to do his shopping.

The duffels were filled with wonderful items: an anorak with coyote fur around the hood; a parka filled with goose down, also with coyote fur around the hood; polypropylene underwear to wick the sweat away from the body and prevent the body from cooling by evaporation; furry mittens with room inside for hands in gloves; bunny boots, two layers of rubber with insulation in between, again protected from dampness; mukluks, Eskimo style soft boots, and mukluk liners; high, lined fireman's boots for the boat and wet ground when the weather was not cold enough for bunny boots; leather gloves and glove liners; wool socks; wool balaclava to go over head and neck and most of the face; wind pants—known as many-pockets pants—made of tightly woven cotton to act as a wind break; insulated liners for the many-pockets pants; wool shirts and wool pants; waffle-weave cotton underwear for flying, because synthetics, which burn easily, are forbidden on all flights to and in Antarctica.

That night, the last on land, I had my first dinner in the officers' mess—the wardroom. Dale Thompson, the executive officer, or XO, a trim, short man in his early forties, presided. He is a graduate of the Coast Guard Academy and a lover of fine wines and cigars. He discussed the merits of Australian wines made from the shiraz grape with the geologist onboard, Jonathan Berg. Though the food was basic institutional fare, the etiquette was formal. Late arrivers asked permission to sit down and requested permission to excuse themselves from the table—"By your leave, XO?"—if they wanted to do so before he was done. The captain had his own mess and dined with invited guests, except on Sunday, when he was a guest in the officers' mess.

After the discussion of wines, the XO—nobody ever called

him by name—pointed out that all U.S. Coast Guard and Navy ships were dry, and had been so since 1862. In fact, he said, the United States had the only dry navy in the world. Even when a ship was docked and receiving local dignitaries for a reception, the captain had to obtain special permission from Washington to serve alcohol. We were served beer once or twice during the trip when we stopped in the middle of the frozen sea. The captain declared ice liberty, and each crewman and passenger was issued two beers, to be consumed on the ice and not to be sold, traded, or given to fellow sailors who might want more than two beers.

We set sail on December 19. From the deck, Coast Guard men, mostly boys, waved to girls on the dock. When the boat started to roll a bit as it moved out into the harbor, I felt a thrill, a rush of exhilaration. I found the sensation of movement, of travel and possibility, to be located not so much in the open sea at the horizon, but in the bow wave. It was a sort of yin and yang, I suppose, the complementarity of boat and wave. Or perhaps it was Schrödinger's Swell. You could not try to know the sea without disturbing it. The sea without a boat cutting through it, whether the boat is given speed by wind or diesel, is like the tree that falls when no one is there to hear it. Photographs, airplanes, remote imaging from satellites were all just that: remote. But here the roll of the decks and the shape of the wave meant that you had somehow entered into a relationship with the sea.

And the sea also made the boat come to life. The ludicrous and distressing details of boat construction, such a bore to landlubbers like me, came to make sense, to resonate with functionality. For instance, the uncomfortably small hatches on the stairs from deck to deck revealed their purpose when crewmen used them to seal off each deck during fire drills.

One day we learned how to fold a life preserver, or, rather, a "personal flotation device," and how to put it on, and which lifeboats we had been assigned to. The next day we learned to get from our rooms to the weather deck and back with our eyes closed, because there are no windows below decks, and if a fire put out the electricity we would have to contend with not only smoke and fear, but total darkness.

I began to enjoy ducking my head and learned to float down the narrow stairs with hands on the rails and feet only tapping the steps. All the drills and order were wonderfully satisfying when set against the threat of the sea. Even rituals of deference and military politesse came to seem a kind of talisman against the potentially overpowering chaos of the ocean. When sailing with friends and relatives I had always been irritated by the idea of stowing everything, lashing it down. But thinking of 40-degree rolls and 75-foot waves, I began to get religion. I began to see that in addition to getting the ship shipshape, one might want to lash oneself down, to become, in manner and behavior, tight and polished, the better to face the liquid, unbound sea.

The *Polar Sea* carried a crew of 140. Its two helicopters had their own aviation group of four pilots (three men and a woman, all officers) and about ten enlisted men. Alda Siebrands, a helicopter pilot who had flown for the army before she flew for the Coast Guard, was the only woman on the ship. Only the officers' quarters allowed for private cabins. The ship was scheduled to be remodeled to allow for enlisted women in the future.

Below the weather deck were the living quarters and below that engines and fuel tanks. Above the weather deck was the flight deck and the bridge, 55 feet above the water. The "aloft con" towered above the bridge like a crow's nest. It was a tiny enclosed space with controls to drive the ship. During icebreaking, the officer who was driving the ship rode in the aloft con, 100 feet above the water, to be able to see where the leads were, how best to navigate through the ice. When the ice became truly troublesome, the captain sent the helicopters out for ice reconnaissance.

My cabin was with the scientific party, all the way aft. It seemed to be located somewhere inside a giant motor. The room looked normal enough. You entered it from one of the common corridors, but inside there was a constant thrum. The room was quite near the screws, which I didn't really notice until we got under way. Once we came into the ice, the bunk would shake and tremble as the screws shattered ice chunks the size of cars.

One of the other noticeable features of the room was that there were no portholes. When all the lights were off, the room was so dark that, as the saying goes, you could not see your hand in front of your face. Warm. Dark. Humming. It was an electric womb.

I had three roommates for the trip to McMurdo: one brand-new Coast Guard ensign, very quiet, and two young New Zealand navy officers whose main interest at first was working out in the ship's exercise and weight rooms, but whose true talent turned out to be sleeping. By the time we reached McMurdo Sound, our destination, the two Kiwis were routinely taking morning and afternoon naps. Since the ensign sometimes worked late watches and caught up on his sleep whenever he could, the room was almost always dark, at any time of the day or night. It was the perfect counterpart to the world above decks where, at the height of the austral summer, it was so light, night and day, as to hurt unshielded eyes.

The head flooded often because of a troublesome plumbing system. I was convinced by the end of the trip that there is no worse job than to be a plumber on a big ship. With the wet floor in the head, all bunks occupied, and the perpetual darkness, the room gradually acquired a swamplike atmosphere. There aren't many places in the Antarctic where you can grow mushrooms. This was one of them.

Reveille was at 6:45, breakfast at 7. I'm not a health fanatic. I like a giant oozing sausage for breakfast as much as the next guy—well, as much as most next guys. On this trip, however, I was completely outgunned. Most of the younger officers and most of the scientists too ate breakfasts that would give the American Heart Association an institutional coronary. By the time I had finished my tour of duty on the icebreaker I became convinced that a career's worth of Coast Guard breakfasts could be as dangerous as combat. A common ensign's breakfast consisted of a cheese omelette, bacon or sausages (sometimes both), pancakes, syrup, cereal, orange juice, and coffee. The omelettes were excellent—not French omelettes, but the sort of huge spilling-over concoctions you get at a good roadside diner. The sausages were pretty good too. I had them once or twice.

Lunch and dinner were neither good nor bad. The standard joke was that each meal had to have three kinds of starch. We often had noodles, rice, and something like potato salad to go with the meat (chicken, pork, lamb, steak, other), vegetables, and salad. It was the sort of food you could get at an old-fashioned neighborhood restaurant that has liver and onions once a week. The fruits and greens for salads were freshly purchased at each port. On the way down to McMurdo, kiwis were plentiful. There were bananas and oranges, fresh lettuce, tomatoes. In the Antarctic these are rare treats. Of course, by the time the ship was on its way back to Chile after the Antarctic tour, the only salad was three-bean.

The diet in movies was also heavy. We seemed to see a lot of Schwarzenegger. Actually there were many other movies, but the Schwarzenegger ones stuck in my mind, perhaps because I had abandoned Arnold after *Conan the Barbarian*, and this trip marked my reintroduction to him. On board I saw *Predator, Running Man, Terminator*, and other classics. Also *Bill and Ted's Excellent Adventure* (a cult favorite particularly favored by the XO) and a lot of teen romances. I could not understand what all these teenage romance movies were doing on an icebreaker, until somebody pointed out to me that the majority of people onboard were, in fact, teenagers.

Above decks, before we encountered the ice, the sea was as gray and remote, as opaque as it could be. There were days of fog, with no birds, when we could see more or less where the sun was, but could not see the sun. The horizon was blurred, as in a drawing done in pale gray charcoal, the boundaries of sea and sky smudged by the artist's thumb. All around us at the edge of vision the dark sea blended into the paler clouds.

The fog may have marked our passage through the Antarctic Convergence, where the cold water of the Antarctic meets the warmer northern water. In the days before the fog, I watched the albatrosses follow the contour of the swells and thought of what a wonderful word that was—"swell." It was not a wave so much as the sea swelling and then going flat. The wide and distant horizon, even when the sun was out, caused a hunger for land, or perhaps for detail. I felt it as an aesthetic loneliness, a need for islands or birds or whales or other ships—any divergent sight in the expanse of sameness.

A few days out, I found the captain, Gary Boyer, on the bridge and began to talk to him about the sea. He was always ready to respond. He gave me a couple of appropriate quotations. I think he may have been saving them, knowing a writer would be coming onboard. One was from Oliver Wendell Holmes: "The Sea is feline. It licks your feet—its huge flanks purr very pleasant for you; but it will crack your bones and eat you, for all that, and wipe the crimsoned foam from its jaws as if nothing had happened." Now *that* was what I had come to the Southern Ocean for—huge, purring flanks, cracked bones, sucked marrow, crimsoned foam. Not to look out on the gray expanse of waves that could be seen from the quarterdeck, but to confront the feline sea.

Another quote he gave me was of unknown origin:

> No matter how important a man at sea considers himself, unless he is fundamentally worthy, the sea will some day find him out. If a wrong move is made at sea, in a critical moment, death may be the penalty for the most simple failure—not only death to one but to many. Incompetence may prevail upon the shore, but at sea sooner or later it is ruthlessly uncovered and utter disaster often follows in its wake.

I was less thrilled by this notion. The quotation was all well and good for experienced sailors, particularly captains, who had to be pretty well up the sea's scale of who is fundamentally worthy to have gotten where they were. But what about inexperienced, first-time sailors, passengers, writers? I had gotten along so far on land. And the world of a writer is a bit like that of a sailor. You're going along just fine, with magazines and book publishers and their editors purring very pleasant, and all of a sudden they're wiping the old crimsoned foam from their jaws. But that's metaphorical crimsoned foam.

Of course, there was little to worry about. My competence was never on the line. The Coast Guard, having a strong instinct for self-preservation, does not let visiting writers fly helicopters, or dive under the ice, or supervise rescue parties. In any operation in which I participated my presence was calculated as a potential liability. I didn't take offense.

The strangest thing about the first leg of our trip was that within a day or two of leaving port it became clear to me that the sea itself, in its watery state, was not of fundamental interest to anyone onboard but me. The Coast Guard paid attention to sea state, of course, as it related to the progress of the ship. But the scientists onboard were geologists, meteorologists, and glaciologists. They were interested in volcanic rock on Antarctic islands, a network of weather stations, and sea ice. No oceanographers, no birders or whale hunters had signed on for this trip. I knew more about seabirds than anyone onboard, which is a statement about their ignorance, not my knowledge. I had come to work the water, and found that on this ship, on this trip, the sea was a road, a means of travel. Without a storm, without a confrontation, as long as the sea licked our feet and purred very gentle for us, it stayed in the background of everyone's attention. On the icebreaker, untroubled time at sea was downtime. In short order everyone was counting the days, and then the hours, waiting for ice.

* * *

We sighted first ice December 22, 2230 hours, 62 degrees 37 minutes south latitude, four days out of Hobart—pizza night. On Saturday nights different groups of crewmen or officers would take turns making pizza in the galley. Ham and pineapple, two standard ingredients of Tasmanian pizza, were almost as popular as pepperoni and peppers. When the announcement of first ice came over the public address system, most of the officers and science party were gathered in the officer's lounge watching *Kelly's Heroes*, the movie in which Clint Eastwood leads a group of misfits in World War II to get some German gold. (The film is most notable for Donald Sutherland in the anachronistic role of a 1960s hippie.) Everyone in the officers' lounge abandoned Clint to run up to the flying bridge, an open-air platform over the bridge itself—what a landlubber might call the roof—to look for ice.

It was still light. At this latitude and this time of year, the sun dipped below the horizon but never really set. Below 66 degrees south, the Antarctic Circle, the sun would stay completely above the horizon for the austral summer. At first there was just a blink of light on the horizon that, as we drew nearer, turned into a slushy band of broken sea ice, then more water, then more ice. With the sea ice, and icebergs in the distance, the first snow petrels appeared, pure white birds with black beaks. The snow petrel flies like a pigeon, curving and swooping in and out of visibility as it passes patches of white ice and dark ocean.

As I watched the snow petrels flicker in and out of sight, the ship approached and then veered away from a bergy bit, a chunk of ice that was bigger than a sofa but smaller than a house. Bill Shultz, chief helicopter pilot onboard, a lieutenant commander, yelled in mock outrage to the officer of the day below us in the bridge: "Hit it, you chicken!"

The next morning the photons were bouncing every which way in a thick fog, to enclose us in a uniformly overbright cocoon. We could see only a few hundred yards. The ship plowed in desultory fashion through brash ice—open water and chunks of melting sea ice running up to tennis-court size. Calvin Trillin once reported a Floridian's definition of a Southern cracker: "He do not care. He flat do not care." Since I read this phrase I have used it over and over again in various circumstances, but it applies to nothing so well as a big icebreaker.

When we hit a snow-covered ice cake with a thunk and a rumble, rising up onto it and sinking through, the ice crumbled into the water off the port bow, breaking into pieces like a crusted surface of confectioner's sugar. Once broken, the ice revealed, under the alluring surface, the dirty, yellow taint of living algae. In the Antarctic life is equivalent to dirt. Around the coastline of the Antarctic continent or the ice edge, or in the ice, wherever there is life, there is filth—the discoloration of algae, or lichen on the rocks, the feces of seals, penguin guano. It often seems on looking at an Antarctic coastline that keeping it unspoiled would mean forbidding access not only to humans, but to all other organic colonizers.

All that day, Sunday, the twenty-third of December, we moved through a whiteout—well, actually a light gray–out. The fog and ice blurred together—photon soup. I learned that a fog can be so bright that it hurts the eyes. The ship began to move more slowly through loose ice that was getting thicker. We were driving through patches of water, bumping some ice floes, crunching others. Jumbled, ragged pressure ridges rose up several feet where the ice had broken and refrozen. One large snow-covered piece of ice slowed the ship almost to a stop before the breaker's weight cracked it.

In the midst of this progress I stood on the bow with two helicopter pilots, one of them Shultz, who was recounting a rescue story from his last Antarctic tour. He was at the point where the helicopters had found the stranded travelers and their disabled ship. He had begun ferrying people to an island where the helicopters had to set down right in the middle of a penguin rookery with the rotor wash bouncing the penguins down the slope. Ralph Hawes, the other pilot, interrupted him and pointed to what seemed to be the horizon, but then again didn't look like the horizon. Perhaps it was a cloud line. Then, suddenly, it dawned on the two pilots that what we were looking at was not the horizon at all but the flat top of a big tabular iceberg only a few ships' lengths in front of us.

Shultz and Hawes started shouting at the officers on the bridge and waving their hands. Seeing them waving, and realizing what they were exercised about, the lookout in the bow started waving to the bridge and pointing to the iceberg as well. I was standing my ground (or deck) to see what happened until I was practically dragged aft by Shultz to get behind some bulkheads. Slowly, in stately fashion, the ship turned, and an announcement came over the public address system in a matter-of-fact military voice informing those who wanted to see icebergs that there was one coming into view about 50 yards off the port side.

Ice, of course, is the *Polar Sea*'s element. The ship may roll and pitch in liquid water, but in solid water it achieves its true nature, something like the way penguins, lumbering and silly on land, reveal the economy and elegance of their design when they enter the ocean. Until we reached McMurdo on January 4 the ship was almost always breaking ice—in sun, in white fog, in zero visibility, with a visibility of 50 miles. The ship's smooth bow and hull would ride up on the ice as its engines forced it forward. The broken chunks would surge up the sides of the bow, then sink down and bob up again as they passed aft toward the screws, three propellers, each 16 feet in diameter, that milled the ice chunks—chopped, shaved, and crunched them, like ice cubes in a Cuisinart.

When the ice got thick and hard, the ship got stronger and louder. The captain ordered the use of the gas turbines (essentially jet airplane engines) instead of the diesels. At a different tempo then—allegro—the ice broke, snapped, popped. The ice cakes plunged down and leaped back up through the aquamarine foam.

Crashing through ice in a big icebreaker offers a kind of hypnotic pleasure. Out on the bow I listened to the ice cracking into 10-ton bites as the fault lines shot out from the ship into the white plain ahead of us. I tried to predict where the cracks would appear, where, when the tension accumulated until it was too great, the undisturbed plain of the frozen sea would simply split apart, yielding to our progress.

After days of foggy whiteout conditions we came into what looked like a war zone. There were no distinguishable ice floes. The field of view in front of the ship was all jagged walls and ridges pushed together. The ice had begun to break up, melt, crack into floes, and loosen. The floes, tossed about by winds and waves, had crashed into each other, throwing up small mountain ridges of ice, as when colliding tectonic plates produced the Himalayas or the Andes. And these ridges had frozen. The temperature had dropped. Instead of forging ahead through the Great Plains, we were now forced to ram mountain range after mountain range. We were not blocked. But we were forced to give up nonchalance. To break through this jumble we had to back and ram, use the turbines, struggle. The captain sent a helicopter out for ice reconnaissance to look for leads, to find a way around the worst of the ice.

But that was unusual. By and large we cut a linear, purposeful course through curvilinear nature. We were not dependent on the wind. We were not stopped by ice. We were not sailing, we were driving. The ship rode up on the ice and cracked it. The ice burbled past the watchers on the quarter deck. As we drove south, the colder, steely blue ice, a meter or two thick, made an audible pop when it broke. Sometimes the ship rode up on a large ice floe and rested, momentarily stopped. We reversed direction, drew back, and then slammed onto the ice again. We passed through places in the Southern Ocean where few human beings had ever been. For days at a time we could see only ice to the horizon in every direction.

The blankness and sameness of the ice and the vastness of the frozen sea tended to concentrate the attention of crew and passengers on the machine in which we traveled. In all the alien expanse of ice here was activity, humanity, fire. Most of the people onboard were longtime lovers of machines. They talked at length and with pleasure about various models of helicopters, aircraft, and icebreakers, enumerating their benefits and drawbacks, the way some men talk about baseball teams, or the way avid birders discuss the field marks of the royal and wandering albatross.

When I first came onboard I was, so I told myself, a fan of the organic as opposed to the mechanical. But as time passed I too was seduced. I spent more and more of my hours preoccupied with the thrusts and shudders of the breaker's passage. I slept near the screws, with my head just about at the waterline, and the noise of propulsion was always with me. After a time I came to rely on it. A modicum of shaking and shuddering and groaning served as the nightly rocking of a giant cradle.

In the end the ship's power was irresistible. There are few things in life that satisfy so completely the desire to drive heavy machinery as an icebreaker. You run it up against Nature and the machine wins, noisily and with much crunching. The ship had an exercise room in the bow, with only a bulkhead between it and the ice. The roar and crash of icebreaking that transmitted itself through the hull into this room was exhilarating. Often, when I used the cross-country ski machine, instead of wearing a Walkman and listening to music to distract myself, I listened to the roar of the ship and the ice. I imagined that I was powering the ship, like a terrier turning a spit. As my heart pounded and sweat dripped into my eyes, I cherished the roar and strode faster.

The difference between me and the rest of the machine-loving crew and passengers was that they had some clear understanding of the mechanics of the machine. I was riding a metaphor. This was no mere ship, but a rich semiotic stew. I had not just hitched a ride with the Coast Guard, I had saddled up the Enlightenment. I was driving the Industrial Revolution, the scientific method, Western technology. I was all four horsemen of an environmental apocalypse bashing through the mystery and apparent chaos of nature, and carrying my narrative along with me.

The ship digressed occasionally, as befits any voyage, any story. But it was by no means an avant-garde machine. It was tradition incarnate—martial, patriarchal, European, sexist, so phallic as to be embarrassing (just like a traditional narrative, perhaps). As we forced our way through the ice I entertained myself with the notion that both the ship and my story were burning a kind of fossil fuel. In one case diesel. In the other the accumulated cultural thrust of countless dead white males.

The sexual metaphor wasn't mine. It was received, not invented. In the ship's store women's panties were for sale and a sample pair was tacked onto the wall with other wares. Written on their aft side, in large letters, was the legend "BACK AND RAM." Nor did the makers of novelty underwear invent the metaphor; the language drips with the sexualization of exploration and conquest. Virgin forests and continents, places *man* has not yet sullied. The South Pole has not been virgin since Amundsen reached her, not even when Scott arrived. Once the land is penetrated our relationship to it changes. Colonizers and developers may no longer open up the land, but they can still rape it.

The imagined maleness of exploring is aggressive, not seductive. Indeed, the progress of the icebreaker, seen in this context, seems monstrous. There is nothing of courtship in its movement; it forces its way. The breaker has none of the delicate dance steps of a sailing ship with wind and water, although the best boat drivers do pick and choose their course, looking always for leads, for softer ice, for the path of least resistance.

But on a larger scale in space and time, the loaded traditions of language fall away. The metaphors become obscurantist baggage, a male fantasy, a case in which truly extraordinary actuality has failed to replace imagination with consciousness. The truth is that when the breaker passes through, the ice re-forms. Taking the long view, or even the medium view, on the scale of seasons, the breaker is no more assaultive than any ship slipping through water in its liquid state. The wake just takes a bit longer to subside.

Sea ice covers, at the maximum, about 7 percent of the earth's surface. In the Arctic Ocean the summer ice cover, at its minimum, is roughly the size of the forty-eight contiguous states, 8 million square kilometers. In the winter it doubles to 16 million square kilometers. In the Antarctic the minimum ice cover is smaller, 3 to 4 million square kilometers. But in the winter it grows to 20 million square kilometers, two and a half times the size of the forty-eight contiguous states, and greater in area than the continent of Antarctica itself.

The growth of the ice is enhanced by the growth of the ice—positive feedback. As the ice begins to grow at the end of summer (at either pole) it reflects more of the sun's heat away from the surface of the ocean than the water does. So, as air temperatures cool, and the ice cover spreads, temperatures close to it drop even more, producing more ice. When the warming starts in the spring, the reverse happens. The warmer the air temperature gets, the more ice melts and the more water is exposed, so the ocean absorbs more heat, thus increasing its temperature even more and hastening the melting of the ice.

In models of future climate change, most of which predict global warming, the biggest changes often appear in the polar regions, but the results may seem paradoxical. The consensus is that warmer global temperatures will bring about more precipitation in Antarctica, since a warmer atmosphere can carry more moisture. Antarctica is now practically a desert, with precipitation—in the form of snow—of 6 to 7 inches. More snow would cause the Antarctic ice sheet to grow, rather than shrink, in initial stages of global warming.

Sea ice is different. Warming should reduce the winter ice cover on the ocean. Sea ice is intimately related to the Southern Ocean's temperature and salinity stratifications, its currents, and its relationship to the world's other oceans. The ice is, after all, not a cover slapped on a pot, but the ocean itself in one of its forms. And, of course, ocean and atmosphere are linked. One cannot isolate individual components of the world's physical systems any more than one can isolate the various forms of life in an ecological system. Nor, of course, can one separate living things from the physical systems.

The Southern Ocean serves, in one capacity, as a global heat sink. Warm water from the Atlantic, Pacific, and Indian oceans flows south into this ocean where the heat is lost to the cold polar atmosphere and to the ice. At the same time the Antarctic bottom water, cooled by the atmosphere and the continent's ice shelves as they flow into the sea around them, moves north to cool the Atlantic, Pacific, and Indian oceans.

During the winter much of the Southern Ocean is covered with ice, blocking the release of heat to the atmosphere. But even deep in the ice pack there are leads and great open spaces of water, called polynyas, in the midst of frozen sea. The best known and most studied of these polynyas was seen in the Weddell Sea in the late winters of 1974, 1975, and 1976; it has not occurred since.[3]

This stretch of open sea in the midst of ice reached a maximum size of 350 by 1,000 kilometers. The vertical temperature structure in a polynya is relatively uniform. So polynyas are essentially huge vertical chimneys of relatively warm water, serving as heat exchangers, while most of the surrounding ocean is covered with ice.

There are also coastal polynyas, created when offshore winds blow surface ice out to sea as it forms. Then more sea water freezes and is in turn blown out to sea. Arnold Gordon, an oceanographer who studies polynyas, calls these coastal ones "sea-ice factories." In the process of freezing, the sea water in these polynyas gives off huge amounts of heat to the atmosphere.[4]

The distribution, formation, and nature of sea ice are all subjects of scientific interest. Naturally, an icebreaker is an ideal platform for some of these studies. The ice men on the *Polar Sea* were Willie Weeks and Martin Jeffries. On any trip to the Antarctic there is a certain amount of competition over who has been to the most remote places, in the worst weather, by way of the most interesting flying machines. Weeks and Jeffries, both glaciologists, had a leg up in this regard even without their stories of fieldwork. They lived and taught in Fairbanks, where they were both at the University of Alaska.

They entertained us with tales of Fairbanks winters, of ice fog in the streets, of gloom and darkness. Then they recounted other odysseys of the North, time spent in Thule, Greenland, and Hopedale, Labrador (which Weeks claimed had the worst weather he had ever seen), and on Northern Ellsmere Island. Weeks was fond of describing glaciology as the last "seriously macho profession." Even when they worked in a lab, it was a freezer. The coldest I got during my three-month sojourn in the South was standing in a freezer at McMurdo Station watching Weeks and Jeffries cutting up ice cores and looking at them under microscopes.

Weeks, gray-bearded, in his sixties, had been everywhere cold in the Northern Hemisphere, played the bass fiddle, and had a generally irreverent view of all aspects of life other than ice and music. He was so much the grand old man of glaciology that in 1988 there was a W. F. Weeks Sea Ice Symposium in San Francisco, with glaciologists attending from around the world. Jeffries, a young, tall, red-haired, self-described "Brit," quiet, with a dry, understated sense of humor, was the junior scientist, but it was his grant they were working on, and so he was the "principal investigator." That means, in the traditional hierarchy of scientific fieldwork, that although Weeks was much the senior scientist (to pretty much anyone in glaciology) he was officially Jeffries's sidekick. Both men were easygoing, however, neither of them much interested in the bureaucratic characterization of their roles, neither given much to ceremony or officialdom.

In fact, Jeffries surprised me with his distaste for rank after our first dinner in the officers' mess. We had been informed by a junior lieutenant straight out of the Coast Guard Academy, and far more impressed by the standing of his superiors than by the stature of any of the scientists, of the accepted protocol at dinner. Although we were not subject to the rules as he was, he seemed to suggest it would be only polite if we were to say "By your leave, sir?" when we wanted to leave the table. Jeffries muttered to me shortly after that dinner, "I'll be damned if I'm going to call anyone 'sir.'"

Because of Weeks and Jeffries the breaker did not just encounter ice when it came our way. We sought it out. Not icebergs, which are formed when the glaciers or ice sheets attached to Antarctica calve or break, losing parts of themselves to the sea. It was the pack ice that interested Weeks and Jeffries, the frozen sea itself.

They were studying the crystalline structure of the ice. Different structures give clues to how the ice is formed. There are several different kinds of sea ice. One is congelation ice, a thin section of which, viewed under a microscope, shows crystals that grow vertically, downward, to form in the shape of columns.

These columns are bottom-heavy, however, since the crystals grow thickest at the farthest extension of their growth. An individual crystal may be as thick as 5 centimeters. Like quartz crystals, one crystal will grow faster than another, cutting out other crystals, sucking up the water molecules. Photographs made with polarized filters of thin sections of ice reveal multi-colored patterns of delicacy and intricacy. The orderly, classical arrangement of congelation ice reflects its origin. It grows in calm waters or underneath ice that has already formed. Ice cover dampens water movement and the effects of the wind.

Frazil ice, also called grease ice or granular ice, is composed of crystals that form in the water and float up and join with other crystals. Many southern explorers have described sailing or steaming through a slushy coating on the water, which is frazil ice in the process of freezing. Congelation ice then grows down from this surface layer. In the Antarctic the thicker the ice, the higher the percentage of frazil ice. This is not true in the Arctic because frazil ice is more likely to form when conditions are rough, when wind and waves are disturbing the water, churning the freezing sea. This sort of disturbance is more common in the Antarctic because the Southern Ocean is so open. The Arctic Ocean is enclosed by land, almost like a vast inland sea.

Weeks and Jeffries showed me dazzling microscopic photographs of frazil ice, a rough composition of apparently disorganized, sharp-edged granules, with none of the lovely columnar organization of congelation ice. It looked like ice that grew out of turbulence and conflict. It embodied a sense of fragmentation and dissonance—an ice for our time.

Platelet ice is somewhere between the first two in crystal shape and overall structure. The crystals are larger than the frazil crystals, but not really columnar. It seems to be the result of supercooling. Water may sometimes be cooled below its freezing point and remain in its liquid state. The fragile equilibrium of this supercooled water is easily disturbed. For instance, an anchor rope in supercooled water, when drawn up, will be encased in ice; the rope offers nuclei on which ice crystals form. Platelet ice, under magnification, is composed of harsh triangular and dagger shapes. Sadly, or perhaps instructively, platelet ice defeated my attempt to create an aesthetics of ice crystals, a semiotics of freezing, to pursue the pathetic fallacy of finding a commonality between nature and human culture even at the microscopic level. This ice suggested no metaphors at all.

One of the most interesting developments in recent years in the study of sea ice has to do neither with the large-scale relation of sea ice to climate nor with the microscopic structure and arrangement of ice crystals. Rather it is the investigation of the microscopic life that thrives in the ice. The first observation of ice algae, of microscopic life living in the ice, seems to have been during the James Ross expedition to the Antarctic in 1841. One of the naturalists observed that populations of diatoms were the cause of discolored icebergs and pack ice.

But marine biologists did not begin seriously to study this phenomenon until about twenty years ago. Since then various researchers have determined that pack ice often has higher concentrations of algae than the water around it. What makes this possible is that sea ice is not simply a block of solid H_2O. It is riddled with brine channels in which all sorts of creatures flourish—diatoms, other algae, bacteria, and small single-celled organisms that feed on the algae.

Most of the algae are adapted not only to low temperatures but to low levels of light. About 10 to 15 percent of the sunlight that strikes the surface of sea ice will reach algae 2 meters deep. If snow covers the ice only 1 or 2 percent of the sun's radiation will reach that depth. Not surprisingly, some common ice algae thrive at light conditions that are 1 to 2 percent of surface intensity. Indeed some algae manage to live through the Antarctic winter, which means they make it through four months of total darkness.

How these algae survive in darkness and the role these ice communities play in the life of the larger ocean are among the unanswered questions about life in the ice. The ice may serve as a kind of nursery for growing algae and other organisms. As it melts in the spring it may seed the water at the ice edge. Both scientists and other observers, like whalers, have noted a spring algal bloom at the ice edge, which draws krill, birds, seals, and whales.

Krill are also an active part of the ice community. They feed on the bottom of ice floes, and birds sometimes congregate in the wake of an icebreaker to feed on krill exposed on the undersurface of the disturbed ice. Krill also move into the ice, entering some of the larger brine channels to forage on the algae.[5]

On Monday, December 24, the day before Christmas, we were socked in. The ship was an island of detail in uniformly bright, off-white fog. On deck I was bombarded by the visual equivalent of white noise. I wasn't suffering sensory deprivation exactly, although I hungered for visual variation and detail, but sensory saturation in a narrow band width.

In this assaultive photon soup I could hear only the hum of the engines and the creaking of the ship. We were in very nearly solid ice, and the ship often stumbled and stopped dead. Then it would back and ram. White snow petrels passed in the near distance like wraiths, as insubstantial as the phantom lights that play across the retina when you close your eyes. Gray Antarctic fulmars were incarnate but indistinct. Pintado, or cape petrels, pigeonlike birds with a black-and-white pattern, produced a shock when they flew close by, like a sudden splash of paint on an empty canvas.

We were just north of the Antarctic Circle. Standing on the flying bridge in the morning I smelled chili cooking for lunch and glanced occasionally at the sun, a small 25-cent piece, a bright disk, but featureless, its blurred halo extending into the fog. The effect was that of being in an eclipse without darkness. All around the boat I saw a jumble of pressure ridges. As I prowled the decks, staring into the all but featureless world, I had the powerful sense of entering new territory. But there was almost no way to give the place specificity. It was like exploring limbo—a near-life experience.

These thoughts impressed on me my responsibility to report back on the experience. What was it like to be surrounded by pack ice? Not in metaphor, not in imagination, not clouded by ancient Catholic images of a forlorn spiritual landscape where the bland souls of unbaptized babies wandered in perpetual blankness, neither condemned to suffer nor granted the exhilaration of God's presence. What was it really like, the actuality?

I tried to lift the fog with the force of my attention, to wring telling details from it. But the longer and harder I looked at the fog and the icescape of pressure ridges, the more it numbed me. The more I struggled to see detail, to define it, the more I drifted into thoughtless staring or extravagant internal meandering. After a while my eye turned back to the ship—to ropes, boats, buckles, shades of paint, decks, aerials, helicopters. And then I went inside for a true jolt of detail—the almost homey roomscape of the officers' lounge, with TV, couches, chairs, a Christmas tree. For a perverse, postmodern experience I could always stretch out on a couch—during the day the officers were mostly working—tune the TV to the channel that picked up the image from the bow's camera, and watch the uniform icescape on television.

We were approaching the Balleny Islands, about 270 kilometers northeast of Cape Adare on the coast of Victoria Land. The Ballenys, discovered in 1839 by John Balleny, an English sealer, are made up of five large volcanic islands and several smaller ones. They form a northwest-southeast chain about 200 kilometers long, and the individual islands were named for partners in the firm that financed Balleny's expedition. In the afternoon we passed Young Island and some grounded icebergs.

The weather began to clear and the ice took on the appearance of a white cake on which someone had dropped lumps of hard sugar in random lines and heaps and dusted them over with confectioner's sugar. Where ice was broken this image was disturbed by a slash of black water, a lead for the ship to follow. And in some spots pieces of broken ice in side view showed a cross section of blue so clear that it seemed to have its own light.

At 6 P.M. a helicopter lifted off from the flight deck. This is what we had been waiting for, weather clear enough to fly. Jonathan Berg, the geologist onboard, was off to collect volcanically expelled remnants of the earth's crust. The helicopter rose, tilted to one side, and faded quickly into the distance.

On the starboard quarterdeck Jeffries and Weeks were being loaded onto a platform and swung over the deck onto the ice to enable them to drill cores, ice cylinders about 6 inches in diameter and up to 10 or 12 feet deep. Jeffries and Weeks used an auger that they had to turn by hand, with arm and shoulder power. From the deck I watched them drill a core, slice it into segments, record the temperature for each segment, and then put the chunks in plastic tubs. Later they would allow the samples to melt and then test the resulting water for salinity, which often varies along the length of a core. For instance, the longer sea ice remains frozen, the less salt is left in the ice. Weeks and Jeffries then drilled another core next to the first, which they would keep frozen for later examination at McMurdo.

After watching them for a while I wandered over to the port side. In a moment the tenor of the trip changed. The subtleties of the minimalist, monochromatic landscape had disappeared. Instead I saw a spreading brown stain, ugly, and smelled the odor of diesel. One of the crew told me that thousands of gallons of diesel fuel had been lost, that one of the fuel tanks in the hull had leaked. A light snow was falling, the snowflakes landing on the slick in the water.

Immediately I asked the marine science officer what was going on. He didn't know. After waiting for him to get back to me with the answer, I went to the captain on the bridge, who told me he also didn't know exactly what had happened. He confirmed that there had been a fuel leak and that his men were working on it. He said he would give me details when he had them, and when he was sure that he had an accurate account of the leak. As he was talking to me an idea came to him. Why wasn't I out on the ice with Weeks and Jeffries? Didn't I want to go? Well, yes, I said, I suppose I did. In fact I had tried earlier to convince the operations officer, Lieutenant Jorge Arroyo, known generally as Ops, to put me on the platform with the two scientists. He had refused my request. Well, said the captain, let's get you out there. No sooner said than done.

As suddenly as I encountered the diesel spill, I was off the ship and on the ice, still trying to figure out how things had moved so fast. It was warm out, above freezing. Weeks and Jeffries were sawing ice cores. I could see Buckle Island off in the distance about 5 or 10 miles, with sunlight shining on it, the glacier and rock lit as if by divine energy.

Weeks and Jeffries continued to work away diligently at drilling and sawing ice. I didn't disturb them with news about the leak. Even when they learned about it they were not terribly distressed. Each scientist onboard had his discrete project. Each project was limited. There were no generalists, as is the case in all of science now. Each researcher has a small corner of knowledge to tend. The other passengers onboard were concerned about the spill, but no one else took it quite as personally as I did. None of their research projects, after all, were compromised by a few thousand gallons of leaked diesel fuel.

For me, having been musing about the ship thrusting through the ice, and having come to the conclusion that at least we were having safe sex with the ice pack, the diesel demanded a reimagining of our progress. The fuel would disappear. This was not a massive oil spill. And the lost algae and krill, if there were any, could not have any serious effect on the Southern Ocean. But that wasn't the issue. Other ships came through the ice. Other ships traveled the Southern Ocean, fishing, or carrying scientists or tourists. Other accidents happened.

As any archbishop could have told me, the only guarantee of perfect safety was abstinence. The world does not permit libidinous reveling without consequence, whether the revels are sexual or mechanical/industrial. The fuel leak interrupted what seemed, in the face of the ugly brown stain, an antiquated, absurdly disingenuous reverie. Rendering a sentimental travelogue of nature's wonders while splashing through the sea with a million gallons of fuel was offensive.

On Christmas day the ship was still leaking fuel. What had happened, I learned, was this: The ship's engines were cooled by seawater, and a pipe that discharged the cooling water back into the ocean ran through one of the fuel tanks that lined the hull. The joint at the meeting of pipe and hull had come loose, and the captain was sending divers in dry suits into the water, which was below freezing. He still did not know how much diesel has been lost and over how long a period.

Christmas was not canceled because of diesel leakage. The scientific party had turkey dinner in the officers' mess with the captain present as a guest of the XO. And the entire crew was granted ice liberty. The ship was moored, which is to say it had driven itself into the ice and stopped, and stairs were set out from the hull to the ice surface. Everyone went out onto the ice to walk, take photographs, play Frisbee and ice football. The weather was near freezing and the sun was out, a lovely Antarctic day. All in all it was your typical holiday, much like a day in the park, except that we were at the Antarctic Circle, playing games on the surface of the sea, and the engineers onboard ship were frantically trying to figure out exactly how the leak had happened, how much was gone, and how much they could recover with a hose over the side sucking up as much diesel as it could.

Two days later, on the twenty-seventh, I toured the ship's engine compartment, Nibelheim to the ice's Asgard. Each of the ship's six diesel engines was the size of a small truck and built on the long lines of a railroad engine. Each diesel engine used

500 to 600 gallons of fuel per hour. The three turbines, if all were going at full speed, used 4,000 gallons of fuel an hour. The engines powered electric motors that turned the shafts, which looked to be 3 to 4 feet in diameter. Two turned clockwise. One turned counterclockwise. The pitch of the propeller blades was adjustable. To reverse, or change speed, the engineers adjusted not the speed at which the shafts turned but the orientation of the blades. Although the engine rooms were huge and noisy, with immense machines, they had a sense of order and neatness that was the exact opposite of the engine room scenes in, say, *Das Boot* or *The African Queen.*

That afternoon history repeated itself absurdly, confirming the notion that all events play first as tragedy and second as farce. It would be absurd to call the leak a tragedy, but the reprise was certainly comical. I was on the bridge when a call came down from the aloft con. The officer who was driving the ship often used the aloft con when we were in the ice to get a better view. He reported that we had lost a barrel of helicopter fuel overboard. The captain immediately issued orders to turn back and retrieve it.

At once there was confusion. Was it a fuel barrel after all? It couldn't be, because the bosun said fuel barrels are always stored in pairs, and if one fell overboard the other would too. Somebody fixed on the object with binoculars and declared it a trash barrel. Then there was the question of whether it was plastic or metal. Metal would sink or rust, and could be left behind, but plastic was forever. By the time the determination was made that the offending barrel was metal, it was too late. The ship was already going back for it.

Turning around a 400-foot icebreaker in solid ice is no small task. The barrel was about a mile behind us when we started to turn. It took twenty minutes to get back to it by making a wide arc and proceeding at walking speed. It took another twenty minutes to get the barrel. The bosun and one of the bosun's mates took turns throwing a grappling hook at the barrel. Their efforts reminded me of the amusement park game in which the player manipulates a grasping claw that is dropped on a pile of trinkets. I watched from the bridge with the captain and the officers in charge, who commented, as the attempts continued, on the relative skill of the bosun and the mate. It was the mate who snagged the barrel in the end, and they both hauled it onboard, saving the Antarctic from a trash can.

It turned out that a crew member had thrown the barrel overboard with a rope attached in an attempt to get slushy ice water for an initiation ceremony being staged on the flight deck. He let it fill with slushy water (the ship was moving only a knot or two) and, when he tried to haul it up, was all of a sudden reminded of how much a trash can full of water weighs. This realization caused a sudden attack of common sense, and he let go of the barrel.

This particular misjudgment seems to be something of a tradition for young seamen. My first night onboard the captain told a similar story. When he was a younger officer on a smaller ship somewhere near Puerto Rico, a sonar tech—everyone at the table nodded knowingly at the mention of sonar techs, who apparently are not known for good sense—threw a bucket on a rope over the side to get water. He had thought about what he was going to do and had tied the rope to his hand so he wouldn't lose the bucket. That part of the plan was sound; he didn't lose the bucket. But since the ship was doing 15 knots the tech was yanked overboard as soon as the bucket hit the surface. Both bucket and tech were quickly and safely retrieved.

The initiation ceremony that occasioned the loss of the trash can was scarcely less sensible than the bucket episode. The occasion was the baptism of new red nose sailors, so-called because they had crossed the Antarctic Circle for the first time. Those who wanted their passage certified showed up on the flight deck, in the elements, in nothing but long underwear. Each candidate waited his turn to dive into an inflatable boat (a Zodiac) full of ice water (dipped up, with a bucket this time, from the sea). The air temperature and the water temperature were both below freezing. The Zodiac was about 2 feet deep. Everyone who dived in got cold and wet. A few of the crew members came out bruised and bleeding. It was the busiest day of the cruise for the ship's medical officer, but there were no serious injuries, so the ceremony was considered a success.

That evening I talked to the captain in his cabin about the fuel loss. The engineers had been investigating the leak and the divers had been down in the water. He had a preliminary idea of what had happened. The first indication that something was wrong had been on Christmas Eve, when a lookout saw what he thought was an oil sheen behind the ship. At that point the ship's engineers started checking the tanks, and found one, a 30,000-gallon tank, completely full, even though the tanks were never filled more than 95 percent with fuel.

When the engineers tested the contents of the tank, which a few days before had 100 percent fuel, it read as 100 percent water. That would mean that the ship had lost 30,000 gallons of diesel. The tank had a 4-inch diameter discharge pipe running through it, a pipe through which seawater that had been sucked in as a coolant for the engines was discharged. The pipe went through the hull near the bottom of the tank, and it was apparently at the point where it was welded to the hull that the sea had leaked in and the oil out.

However, the captain said, the outlet was at the bottom of the tank and diesel was lighter than water. So it didn't make sense that all the fuel had been lost. The engineers pumped the contents of the damaged tank into another empty tank. Since the leaking tank was still open to the sea, which kept coming in, the pumping yielded 80,000 gallons, which the engineers then started running through a separator, to strip the water from the fuel. As they reclaimed fuel, the estimate of what had been lost decreased from 30,000 to 15,000 and then to 5,000 gallons. A few hundred of those gallons had been retrieved from the ice with a hose sucking up the dirty water. (By the time of the trip back from Antarctica, the captain's investigation and report were complete, and the amount he finally reported as lost to Coast Guard authorities was 3,000 gallons.) The captain also told me that diesel was a light, colorless, highly refined fuel, like kerosene, and would not have left the brown stain, which must have been rust or algae.

The captain had sent a helicopter to backtrack seven hours of the ship's transit. The helicopter crew saw no sheen on the water. The last time the tank had been checked was November 30, but the captain thought that whatever fuel had been lost was lost on the day before Christmas. He kept the ship 5 miles downwind of Sabrina Island, the nearest land, and that 5 miles was ice-covered, so he anticipated no damage to life on shore. I spoke to the National Science Foundation representative onboard the ship, Bernard Lettau, who was serving as the leader of the scientific contingent on this cruise, and he confirmed that the captain had reported the leak as required to the Coast Guard. The captain later gave me the report to inspect.

Lettau said it was possible that the leak could cause some damage to storm petrels. But it was in no way comparable to, say, the spill that occurred near Palmer Station when the Argentine ship *Bahia Paraiso* foundered and lost 150,000 gallons of fuel in February 1989 (also the year of the Exxon *Valdez*). Scientists are still tracking penguin populations and other animal life near Palmer Station to see if there will be any permanent effect.

That is probably the best-known environmental accident in the Antarctic and, oddly enough, it occurred while I was on my first Antarctic trip. In fact we were near Palmer Station at the very time that the ship ran aground. An editor I worked with at the *New York Times* as a freelancer wired me to see if there was anything I could file on the spill, and I tried to convince the captain of the cruise ship to send me over in a Zodiac with some of his crew—to no avail. He did radio to Palmer to see if assistance was needed, but the answer was no. Our ship passed within a few miles of Palmer, so close that there was a sheen on the water in places as we passed.

Two trips to the Antarctic, the least spoiled, most remote place on earth, and two fuel spills—I was batting a thousand.

As we left the spill behind us and drove through the ice toward McMurdo, the days and nights were now blindingly white. The world above decks had become the Daylight Zone—lost cousin of the Twilight Zone. Below decks, in the twilight of windowless rooms and corridors, there was a cavelike comfort. Above decks—whiteout. Usually one thinks of darkness as being disorienting. Here brightness was disorienting. In these conditions helicopters sometimes turn upside down and crash because the pilots can't tell where the ground is. In 1980 an airplane of tourists crashed on Mount Erebus, killing 257 people—everyone onboard. There was nothing wrong with the plane; the pilot lost his bearings.

I took two helicopter flights on this leg of the trip. One was a quick flight to observe the ice. On the other we flew to a 1,000-foot-high ridge on Franklin Island. Adelie penguins nested up to 800 feet on the island's steep, clifflike sides. Above the island a crowd of skuas, perhaps a hundred of them, circled in the sky. The two pilots; a crewman; Jonathan Berg, the geologist; and I walked along the ridge, away from the helicopter, looking for rock samples and nearly trampling skua nests. The nests were simply pairs of eggs left unprotected on the rocky ground. Not that there was any reason to protect them, until we showed up. The skuas attacked us immediately, diving straight at our heads. I had dodged them before, on the Antarctic peninsula, so I knew that the birds buzzed the highest point you offered them, so if you raised your hand above your head, they buzzed your hand. One of the helicopter pilots was not familiar with skuas. He kept dodging, twisting and bending his neck to get his head out of the way until he got a crick in his neck. He had to take muscle relaxants to get rid of it and, under military rules, was not allowed to fly for several days.

On the morning of December 30 I went up on deck expecting to see more sea ice. Instead I found blue open water, huge tabular icebergs, porpoising penguins, and in the distance the coast of Victoria Land, the western boundary of the Ross Sea. The land had black, basalt cliffs, reddish in spots where the rock had oxidized. The water surface was metallic, like that of a car. Adelie penguins off the bow flashed white like trout showing their pale bellies as they dart and twist while feeding on aquatic insects. Other Adelies dove off the ice floes as we passed.

We celebrated New Year's Eve without alcohol, but with bingo. The party invitation piped over the public address system specified appropriate attire. "Dress is Antarctic Casual. You can wear what you want. But you must wear something." The oldest crew member, a master chief of undetermined antiquity, made an appearance as Father Time. The youngest, a seventeen-year-old sea scout with a tougher beard than I had, appeared in a giant diaper as the New Year.

The next day we stopped at the Italian station at Terra Nova Bay. In color-coordinated blue, red, and gray, the modular buildings had the Euro-chic look of a giant Lego set. There were skuas here too, the civilized sort that preyed on garbage as well as penguin chicks and fish. Among skuas, chicks compete for parental attention, as do human young, but among skuas the attention comes in the form of food. Consequently the loser dies. I have heard this conflict, among penguins, described as obligatory sibling murder. While we were at Terra Nova I watched two chicks and their parents, just to the side of a gravel road, enact this common drama. The bigger chick pecked and bullied the smaller one, chasing it away. The parents paid no attention. Come on, I kept thinking, you lousy birds, run after the little one, help it, give the big one a peck and teach it a thing or two.

No such luck; skuas have a resolutely free-market approach to chick rearing. Might makes right; the bigger bird got the prize, a small fish. The little one would presumably soon starve and die, and no one except a sentimental tourist would give it a second thought.

On January 3, after several days of cruising through open water, we arrived at the ice edge—the boundary of landfast ice that blocked entry to the base at McMurdo. The ship stopped briefly, as if to savor the moment. Breaking this ice, after all, was the primary reason for the trip. The *Polar Sea* had traveled from Seattle to cut a channel in this ice. A few miles off to port the Greenpeace ship *Gondwana* stood silently. On our starboard side the Transantarctic Mountains rose in the distance. Groups of penguins and seals lounged on the ice.

This patch of frozen sea that we faced was bounded by land or the thick Antarctic ice sheet on three sides. It could not be moved aside by the hull of the breaker; it could only be broken and then milled by the propellers. There was no great ceremony as we cracked the edge, just a flurry of penguins and seals heading for safety. For the first night we moved through the plain of ice smoothly, cutting a huge semicircle in hopes that the wind would blow north from McMurdo and push the ice out into the open Ross Sea.

By morning the going had gotten more difficult. We now strove straight toward McMurdo, crawling along at 1 knot, stopping often to back and ram. The supposed power of the *Polar Sea* seemed considerably less than what was claimed for it. The several ranges of the Transantarctic Mountains took on the look of a fierce fairy-tale kingdom, a white version of the Land of Mordor perhaps, or Narnia under the ice queen's reign. Except that there was no real feeling of malevolence to the ice or the landscape, just the impression of force and elegance. The mountains loomed impersonal, absolute, like winter itself. The sky, a vast shallow bowl, rushed down to the horizon as the ice rushed up, catching the mountains in between.

Against this background the *Polar Sea* made its mechanical progress, with all three turbines fired up and the whole ship vibrating as it crawled along at a knot or a knot and a half. On the morning of January 5, we reached the McMurdo ice pier. We had carved out enough open water the night before to maneuver toward the pier. The first leg of our journey was over. McMurdo was spread out before us in all its glory, like a giant, jumbled construction site.

Chapter 3

SEALING

Thinkers and explorers had talked of a southern continent since the time of the ancient Greeks. By the time the European maritime expansion had begun in the fifteenth century, the question was not just what land, if any, was there, but did it offer anything on which an adventurer could turn a profit?

Unlike the Arctic waters, the Southern Ocean was left largely fallow until European explorers arrived. Neither the Fuegians nor the natives of the Hawaiian Islands nor the Maoris plied the seas surrounding Antarctica enough to call them their own. The cold southern seas and the isolated, unpopulated islands lost in them remained almost completely untouched and unexploited until the English, French, Norwegians, and other Europeans began to sail ever farther south.

Magellan wended his way through the straits that bear his name above Tierra del Fuego in 1520. No one sailed the waters south of the southernmost part of South America until Sir

Francis Drake was blown south to 56 degrees latitude in 1578 after going through the Strait of Magellan. He was the first to glimpse the tip of South America—Cape Horn—and to experience the dangerous waters that would become as infamous as any on the globe. Today the Horn is still dangerous, but when the weather is good tourists land on Cape Horn in rubber boats and clamber up a rickety wooden staircase to the Chilean weather station at the top, where they can purchase patches for their coats and listen to the hee-haw of jackass penguins in the high tussock grass.

The passage between Cape Horn and the Antarctic peninsula is now known as the Drake Passage. Through those waters ships "round the Horn." Although Drake was the first person to sight the Horn, he had already passed to the Pacific, so he was not the first to round it. He continued his journey, as explorer or pirate, depending on whether you speak English or Spanish, up the coast of South America and on as far north as Oregon.

The first ship to round the Horn was captained by Willem Schouten and carried Isaac le Maire. They made the passage in 1616, and le Maire named the Cape for the Dutch town of Hoorn. The Dutch were among the greatest sailors of that time. In their trade with the East Indies they discovered Australia in 1606. In 1642 and 1653 other Dutch explorers discovered Tasmania and New Zealand.

While the Dutch concentrated on trade, Portugal, Spain, Britain, and France were also exploring the southern waters, finding and frequently losing a variety of southern islands like Bouvet and Kerguelen. In 1700 Great Britain's royal astronomer, Edmund Halley, after whom the comet is named, sailed south in the 52-foot-long *Paramour* to chart unknown territory between Cape Horn and the Cape of Good Hope. His ship sailed near South Georgia, viewing penguins and icebergs, and then turned back.

All of these voyages were in the service of trade and exploration, the search for new land. Until late in the eighteenth century the bounty of the Southern Ocean itself lay fallow, untouched by commercial exploitation.

You might call Captain James Cook the father of the Southern Ocean. He was not the first to round the horns of Africa or South America. All that had been long done by the time he made his first expedition to look for Terra Australis, the Southern Continent. But he sailed the southern seas as no one else had, and his discoveries opened the way for the first commercial harvests of the ocean's riches.

Cook was an eminently practical man with little formal education. He had begun sailing as a youth, worked his way up to the position of mate on a coastal coal ship, and joined the Royal Navy at age twenty-one. He enlisted as a seaman and finished as master of the *Pembroke*, a sixty-four-gun ship. He set out on his first voyage of exploration in 1768 in a refurbished coal ship like the ones he had first worked on. This ship, the *Resolution*, was only 110 feet long and 35 feet wide, with a shallow draft and no special protection for the wooden hull against ice. That voyage included Tahiti, New Zealand, and Australia.[1]

On his second voyage he circumnavigated Antarctica. He never sighted the continent, but he did find icebergs and bitter cold, which he reported as evidence of an icy land to the south. He was the first to cross the Antarctic Circle, which he did several times on this trip. One of his journal entries from December 26, 1773, at 65 degrees 15 minutes south latitude, reads: ". . . in the morning the whole sea was in a manner wholly covered with ice, 200 islands and upwards, none less than the Ships hull and some more than a mile in circuit were seen in the compass of 5 miles, the extent of our sight, and smaller pieces innumerable."[2]

One example of Cook's careful practicality was his prevention of scurvy. In his day this scourge was entirely preventable. Nonetheless, some captains lost huge numbers of men to it.

Three ships with 961 men left on one circumnavigation in 1740; by 1744, when the ships returned, 626 had died, most from scurvy.[3] Not on Cook's ships. He paid attention to the knowledge that was already available. As early as 1593 Sir Richard Hawkins used citrus to prevent scurvy. A. Grenfell Price writes in the introduction to a selection of Cook's journals: "In 1617 James Woodall published in his book *The Surgeon's Mate* a strong plea for the use of lemon juice to combat the disease, and it seems clear that for many years thinking seamen realized the importance of citrus and of fresh foods."[4]

Cook loaded up on fresh vegetables and fruit whenever he could. He tried a number of dietary supplements, such as sauerkraut, spruce beer, and inspissated beer—that is, beer thickened by evaporation. He emphasized cleanliness, dryness, and warmth for his seamen. And in three long voyages he didn't lose a single man to scurvy on the ships he commanded. Price writes: "James Cook rose to the heights of supreme achievement by great ability, great courage, great determination, great capacity for hard work, and the power to take infinite pains."[5]

He was not only forceful and practical, but clever. On his first voyage, his seamen would not eat "Sour Krout," as he called it. So he had it served to the officers and let the men take it or not. Within a week he had to set a limit on how much Krout the seamen were allowed.

On that first voyage he observed the habits of the Tahitian natives, in particular the sexual freedom they enjoyed. He apparently did not succumb to temptation, but no one else onboard his ships seemed to have such restraint. Cook did not interfere with his men in their pursuit of pleasure. However, he was not about to indulge desertion, nor was he particularly enlightened in dealing with the Tahitians. When it came time for his expedition to leave he met a mini-rebellion with force—against the Tahitians. Two of his crew escaped to the mountains with their new wives, and Cook got them back by taking local chiefs hostage.

On his second voyage he set out to search for the great Southern Continent, though at first he did not believe it existed. He departed in July 1772 from Plymouth and sailed first to Africa. In November he set off to the Southwest. On November 24 he wrote: "Many Albatross about the Ship, some of which we caught with Hook and line and were not thought dispiseable food even at a time when all hands were served fresh mutton."[6] Killing albatrosses was never considered bad luck, as some landlubbers think. It was shooting them that was forbidden, and still is. One day at the end of my icebreaker voyage, crossing the Pacific to Chile, everyone onboard got a chance to shoot skeet off the port flight deck. There were albatrosses in the air, and the captain reminded us that anyone who shot one would have to answer to him. He wasn't smiling when he said it.

As Cook went farther south, he reported seeing many whales, penguins, and Ice Birds (snow petrels), and much ice as well. The day after Christmas, at 58 degrees 31 minutes south, he passed through several fields of broken ice. "The Ice in some other of the loose fields appeared like Corral Rocks, honey combed and as it were rotten and exhibited such a variety of figuers that there is not a animal on Earth that was not in some degree represented by it."[7]

On a day when there were strong gales, fog, snow, and sleet, and the rigging was covered with ice and the air "excessive cold," he wrote that "the Crew however stand it tolerable well, each being cloathed with a fearnought jacket, a pair of Trowsers of the same and a large cap made of Canvas and Baize, these together with an additional glass of Brandy every Morning enables them to bear the Cold without Flinshing."[8]

On January 14 he crossed the Antarctic Circle, the first ever to do so, and on the eighteenth decided it was time to head back north. "The Ice was so thinck and close that we could proceed no further but were fain to Tack and stand from it. From the mast head I could see no thing to the Southward but Ice."[9]

After going on to New Zealand and then Tahiti, Cook returned to the Antarctic again, reaching latitude 71 degrees south in longitude 106 degrees west on January 30. It would be fifty years before anyone got that far south again.[10] He returned to the Pacific, and in 1774 and 1775 explored the area around Cape Horn and continued east. He discovered the island of South Georgia, which he found grim and forbidding. He also found fur seals there and on other islands, and his reports of their rookeries brought the first wave of hunters south.

Cook was convinced by his explorations that there was indeed land further south. He reasoned that the "Ice Islands," as he called them, did not form at sea. Land had to be their source, but Cook did not expect anyone to reach it. "The risk one runs in exploaring a Coast in these unknown and Icy Seas is so very great that I can be bold to say that no man will ever venture farther than I have done and that the lands which may lie to the South will never be explored."[11]

In February, planning to return home, he reported: "I have now made the circuit of the Southern Ocean in a high Latitude in such a manner as to leave not the least room for the Probabillity of there being a Continent unless near the Pole and out of the reach of Navigation."[12] He thought furthermore that any southern land would be useless. Even the lands he had found, such as South Georgia, he described as "Lands doomed by Nature to everlasting frigidness and never once to feel the warmth of the suns rays, whose horrible and savage aspect I have no words to describe: such are the lands we have discovered, what may we expect those to be which lie more to the South?" He went on: "whoever has resolution and perseverance to clear up this point by proceeding farther than I have done, I shall not envy him the honour of the discovery but I will be bold to say that the world will not be benefited by it."[13]

On his next voyage, after being honored in England, Cook discovered Hawaii, traveled up the northwest coast of North America, and was killed by Hawaiian natives. He had taken a chief hostage again, like a chess master returning to his favorite ploy. This time the gambit failed.

Cook's journals, published in London in 1785, specified the main habitats of southern fur seals. He printed charts that showed the location of South Georgia. He noted the presence of seals in Patagonia. He also located, to the benefit of seal hunters, Prince Edward, Marion, and Crozet islands, and Kerguelen.

On the basis of Cook's records sealing vessels took sail from America to the Falklands and the offshore islands of Chile. There was money to be made, and one can sense, in the captains' logs of the time, the thrill of taking grave risks and winning fortunes. You can also see, in the way a movie shows an accident about to happen in slow motion, the impending collision of European merchants, traders, and sailors with an untouched ocean.

Sealing had, of course, been going on since prehistory. Stone Age clubs and harpoon points have been found in northern France. The Eskimos hunted seals, made carvings of them, and identified the seal with a powerful spirit. The Greenland Eskimos (Angiut) had wood harpoons with ivory points carved from walrus tusks. The Eskimos used whale baleen to fasten the points to the harpoons and made their harpoon lines from sealskin.

With something like this sort of sophisticated but limited technology, so-called primitive men hunted seals on the northern coast of Europe, in Asia from Japan north, in Arctic North America and Greenland. The skins made waterproof leather. The fur was insulation. The blubber could be burned in lamps. The sealers tended to kill the young, sparing the older breeding seals.

In northwestern Europe seal hunting gradually diminished in importance as Europeans became farmers, but people still supplemented their livelihood with seal hunting. They used pikes and nets in the Arctic and the Hebrides. In sites where sealing had been going on for a very long time, the communities regulated the hunting themselves. On the Danish island of Anholt at the end of the eighteenth century the hunters killed only pups up to a certain age at the beginning of the season. At the end of the season they set out to kill as many old bulls as possible. The community divided the take.[14] In the Southern Hemisphere there had been some small use of seals by native peoples. Commercial sealing started as soon as Europeans discovered seals along the coast of South America. Sealing began in Uruguay shortly after the Spanish explorer Juan Diaz de Solfs discovered the country in 1515. Seals are still hunted there. In South Africa hunting began about 300 years ago.

Within a few years of Cook's explorations and his published reports of fur seal colonies, ships were sailing from England and New England (mostly Connecticut) to the shores and islands of the Southern Hemisphere, including Tristan da Cunha, Patagonia, and the Falklands. The commercial adventurers who went after seals created a boom and bust cycle in the Southern Ocean. Sperm whalers were also searching for their prey in the same waters. These were Yankee square riggers like the *Pequod* in Melville's *Moby Dick.* They rounded the Horn to the warmer seas of the South Pacific or did coastal hunting of whales off the same islands and continents as the sealers. They inflicted damage on whale populations, but the means of slaughter at their disposal were limited. In the twentieth century, with factory ships and fast motorized whale catchers with harpoon guns, whalers came into their own and began to destroy the southern whales wholesale.

Sealers, however, having an easier prey, were able to devastate seal populations from the moment they started to kill them. They had to maximize the return on invested capital, and so they acted under inexorable economic pressure. They spared no efforts to scour the islands and kill every fur seal they could find. And then, in most ingenuous fashion, they would wonder where the seals had gone, and why they didn't return to the islands where the slaughter had occurred.[15]

Many of the sealers were landsmen rather than sailors and shipped on sealing expeditions to try to make a stake to buy a farm when they returned home. They were intent on a quick profit, as were the ship owners. No one looked to the future. Garrett Hardin in his 1968 essay, "The Tragedy of the Commons," puts forward the idea, now frequently heard, that if a resource belongs to no one, no one will protect it. The seals belonged to no one.

In a report on the first American sealers, one historian pointed out that the hunt for fur seals was like a gold rush, and information was closely held. "In some cases the crew was pledged to secrecy, for in the case of the sealing explorer, the vessel was manned by carefully chosen seamen who would share in the returns to an extent unknown to the ordinary seaman."[16] The explorer-mariners who plied this trade became as adept as spies at transferring information and keeping locations confidential. Some of the sealers operated fleets of vessels and set up mail drops and spots to rendezvous in the most remote places.

For instance, when the sealer and explorer Edmund Fanning rediscovered the Crozet Islands and their flourishing, untouched colonies of fur seals, he left a message at Prince Edward Islands for another ship of the same owners. He made a marker of stones, but then buried the record 30 feet away, as predetermined. When the crew for whom the message was meant reached the spot the marker was gone and a hole was in its place. But the papers were safe and sound.[17]

It was a period of high adventure. The ships were not large, less than 50 tons, and they went into "waters feared by naval commanders of the world's greatest maritime nations."[18] The sealers kept pushing the boundaries of the known, going farther south, finding the unknown rookeries. Logbooks and charts were as secret as the Portuguese navigation aids in the 1500s that enabled mariners to get to Japan. Knowledge, like the seal pelts themselves, was held by whoever financed the voyage. Profit was the engine that drove the sealing trade, and the sealers set to the task at hand with a flinty, single-minded New England determination. So armed, in the space of a few decades they all but exterminated the Southern fur seal.

The first known ship to set out to hunt seals rather than pick them up as an added cargo if other ventures allowed was the *States.* It sailed in 1775 and brought back 13,000 skins from the Falklands. The price in New York was 50 cents each. In China the skins brought $5 each.[19] China was the other key to the boom. It was not merely the discovery of seals on their breeding grounds that brought on the rush. Chinese furriers there had developed a new process for making felt from sealskins, and they were paying top dollar for the skins. Ships headed out for two or three years to hunt seals, take them to Canton, trade for Chinese goods, and then return to New England or sail to Europe for yet another trade before coming back.

Having once gone sealing in the southern seas, then on to Canton and back, men did not want to try again. Men from Nantucket to Long Island joined these crews, and they were often left on remote islands for months or years to kill seals. "A sailor's share," wrote the supercargo of the *Neptune* in 1798, "is upwards of twelve hundred dollars, and most of them are calculating to turn farmers."[20] The average voyage generated a sailor's share a half or quarter of that. By investing part of their share, the cash advance, in Chinese goods to sell at home, crewmen could double their money.

At first the sealers knew very little of their prey. Edmund Fanning recounted that on an initial expedition in 1792, neither he nor the ship's master knew which animals were which. They went after sea lions, which are hair seals, not fur seals.

These creatures did not stand and die as fur seals did. Instead, faced with danger, they tore off on their elbows for the water, which could only be reached by going through the sealers. "They immediately rose, and sent forth a roar that appeared to shake the very rocks on which we stood, and in turn advancing upon us in double quick time, without any regard to our person, knocked every man of us down with as much ease as if we had been pipe stems."[21]

Joel Root was the supercargo on a four-year voyage on the *Huron,* which set out from New Haven, Connecticut, in September 1802. He wrote a narrative account of this "sealing and trading voyage" that describes the voyage from beginning to end.[22] After collecting the fur seal pelts they took them to Canton, China, where they sold them for 95 cents each, much less than the profit made by the traders in the voyage of the *States* thirty years earlier, perhaps because the sealers were killing so many animals and producing so many pelts. During the time that the fur seal trade flourished, prices went up and down.

Root considered the 95 cents a good price. His ship then accepted a freight for Hamburg, where the China goods that crew, captain, and owners had bought in Canton were sold. Then the *Huron* went on to St. Petersburg to buy Russian goods for the American market. After sale of his own goods at Hamburg Root had more than $20,000 of his own money. The *Huron* was full with goods bought on company funds. So he chartered another ship for his investment. Root got back to New York safely on October 26, 1806, after four years and nearly two months gone. "On the 30th day of October, 1806, I arrived at New Haven and had the inexpressible joy of finding my wife and children all in health, but the children so much altered that I should not have known them had I met them at any other place than their own mother's fire-side."[23]

Root had made his fortune, as all the investors, captains, and seamen hoped to do on sealing voyages. In 1791 there were about a hundred ships of 200 tons or so, and 3,000 sailors sealing in the Southern Ocean. Most of them hunted on South Georgia or at the southernmost tip of South America in the Strait of Magellan. But from 1792 to 1812 American sealers circumnavigated the Southern Ocean, hunting their quarry on every lonely rock they could find.

The common pattern was extermination, or as close to it as the sealers could achieve. For example, Cook discovered South Georgia on January 17, 1775. In 1790 and 1792 there were two known sealing voyages to South Georgia. By 1800 seventeen ships were hunting seals there, taking more than 100,000 skins. One ship, Edmund Fanning's *Aspasia*, took 57,000. By 1822 James Weddell, noting that 1.2 million skins had been taken from South Georgia, observed that the fur seals there were just about extinct.[24]

Another example of how the trade rose and fell was the situation in the Juan Fernandez Islands 500 miles off the coast of central Chile. There are three islands, and one, Mas Tiera, was the home of Alexander Selkirk, the model for Robinson Crusoe. It had been well-known since 1683 that there were seals on Juan Fernandez, but there was no thoroughgoing slaughter until the end of the eighteenth century. Edmund Fanning came to one of the other islands, Mas Afuera, in 1798, on *Betsey*. He took 20,000 skins and left 4,000 stacked in caves for his return. He also left seven volunteers to continue the killing on this rich ground. Other ships followed, and they too left men there. Gangs of men built shelters and, when their numbers increased, fought over territory. They caught fish, killed goats and wild fowl, and raised vegetables. By one estimate these resident sealers took 3 million skins from the three islands in seven years. By 1807 sealing was not really worth it. By 1824 the islands were abandoned.

The seal hunters had more than one boom. The period from 1789 to 1809 marked the first bloody spasm of mercantile interest. The hunters pursued the seals as in a race, trying to slaughter as many as possible as quickly as possible. The seal stocks were all but destroyed and there was, for a time, a glut of fur seal pelts on the Chinese market.

The next decade, from 1810 to 1820, was marked by a London financial crash in 1809, the War of 1812, and a financial crisis in Canton. Some sealing continued, but at a much slower pace. To the seals this was something of a reprieve, just as in the twentieth century World War II would give the whales of the Antarctic waters a respite from slaughter.

Then came a tremendous revival in the 1820s, with the discovery of the South Shetlands in the Antarctic archipelago just below South America. William Smith, an Englishman, discovered the islands in 1819, setting off the usual rush to slaughter. In the 1820–21 season more than one hundred ships, American and British, hunted these islands. Struggles over turf were not uncommon, and conflicts between British and Americans erupted into fistfights on several occasions. James Weddell, a British sealing captain, estimated that about 320,000 fur seals were killed in the 1821–22 season. In 1829 the H.M.S. *Chanticleer* stopped in the South Shetlands and did not see a single seal.

On the coast of South America some governments effectively regulated the killing of fur seals. But these were rare exceptions to the rule of wholesale, unrestrained harvesting. James Weddell, sealer and explorer, praised the situation in Uruguay, on islands in the River Platte, where the governor of Montevideo enforced restrictions on the seal hunt. He, however, did most of his hunting elsewhere. In 1825 he wrote:

> The system of extermination was practiced, however, at Shetland; for whenever a seal reached the beach, of whatever denomination, he was immediately killed, and his skin taken; and by this means, at the end of the second year the animals became nearly extinct; the young, having lost their mothers when only three or four days old, of course all died, which at the lowest calculation exceeded 100,000.[25]

In the Southern Ocean below the Indian Ocean, Yankee hunters worked many islands, such as St. Paul and Amsterdam. St. Paul was volcanic. There was smoke during the day, and at night, from a ship, one could see fires along the islands' skyline. One early visitor said: "The land then appeared as if covered with a sheet of fire, whilst the illuminated smoke gave that vivid appearance to the sky which generally portends a hurricane."[26] The rocks were black and scarred, the sand beaches a dull gray.

Sealers had an enormous effect on the islands. St. Paul and Amsterdam are both north of the true subantarctic zone. They are isolated and surrounded by stormy seas. Neither has a good harbor, and each has only one anchorage. When sealers first arrived in 1789 the islands were covered with coarse grass. In August 1791 St. Paul was somehow set on fire. Amsterdam also burned at this time, either set afire by sealers or because of volcanic action. In 1792 French explorers said the eastern side of island was burning in a "forest fire so hot that the ship had to stay to the windward of it."[27] In another sighting in February 1793 Amsterdam was on fire in several places.

One chronicler of the fur trade wrote:

> the transient sealers . . . decimated the original flora and fauna through repeated carelessness with fire and through the introduction of new species. On the rare occasions that these islands are sighted and visited today, their drab brown vegetation bears only limited resemblance to the green "verdure" reported by their first discoverers and their first settlers. Once they were green, now they are brown, desolated and despoiled.[28]

The sealers often had to try many different locations, particularly during one of the low points of the boom and bust cycle. The *Pickering*, a brig captained by Samuel B. Edes, set out from Boston in 1817. Edes tried the Falklands, Staten Island (off South America), Tierra del Fuego, South Georgia, the Sandwich Islands, Gough, Marion, Desolation, and Marion again for sea elephants. He found no good fur seal grounds.

The *Pickering*'s cabin boy, William Phelps, wrote an account of the voyage. He describes fur sealing, and then how he was left with five men, one a Chinese cook, on Marion. Three drowned in the first month. Edes put a new crew of eight on the island, gave them provisions to last a year, and promised to come back and fetch them and the oil they had gotten from elephant seal blubber in nine months. He came back two years later.

Phelps also described what the actual experience of killing fur seals was like:

> The fur seals are. . . of the average size of a large Newfoundland dog, they have a thick, rich, beautiful fur, about an inch long, of a light brown color, covered with a coat of shiny black hair, or silver gray; they have a head resembling that of a greyhound, are very rapid in the water, can leap their length on shore, and make their way over slippery rocks faster than a man can. They come onshore for the same purposes as the elephant.
>
> We killed them with clubs. A single blow across the nose is sufficient to bring down the largest, when they are finished with the touch of a knife under the flipper; the knife is then passed round the head and flippers, and the skin being slit from the head to tail, in front, it is taken off with much ease. When taken to our rendezvous, the skins were beamed with a currier's knife, and stretched out on the ground in proper shape to dry, fourteen pegs being put in each skin.[29]

The sealers proved to be explorers as intrepid as any of the adventurers who traveled to Antarctica for "purer" motives. Indeed the sealers are sometimes credited with being the first people to set foot on the Antarctic continent. It was the season of 1820–21. The South Shetland Islands were the site of intense competitive sealing. The names of the New England sealing captains who hunted the South Shetlands that season are legendary: Edmund Fanning of New London, Connecticut, who wrote *Voyages Round the World*, led one expedition; and another was led by Nathaniel B. Palmer, captain of the *Hero.* By American tradition, Palmer was the discoverer of the Antarctic peninsula, called Palmer Land by the United States and the home of Palmer Station, one of three U.S. research bases in Antarctica. Palmer has also given his name to a research icebreaker owned by the National Science Foundation, the *Nathaniel B. Palmer.*

One writer, Edouard Stackpole, has offered evidence that sealers from Connecticut were the first to land on the continent.[30] His claim concerns the *Huron,* out of New Haven, whose captain was John Davis. The *Huron*'s tender, *Cecilia,* a schooner-rigged boat called a shallop, was built in the Falkland Islands. On the way south it was exploring and hunting for seals when, on the morning of February 7, 1821, Captain Davis sighted land and put a party on shore. This was in the neighborhood of the Gerlach Strait; Stackpole is sure that they landed on the Antarctic peninsula itself, not on an island.

Fur seals are eared seals. Their limbs are more defined than those of the true seals—they can run on their elbows and they are probably descended from a different line of mammals than the true seals. The elephant seal is one of the true seals. Its hind legs don't stick out from its body. Its front legs are flippers, with no elbow pronounced enough to run on. The result is that, instead of an amphibious dog, it looks like an enormous slug. Other true seals of the Southern Ocean include the deep diving Weddell seals, which usually dive 200 to 400 meters and can go to 800 meters and stay down as long as eighteen minutes; the crab eater seals, which actually eat krill and underwent a big population surge when baleen whales (also krill eaters) were killed in huge numbers in the earlier part of this century; the leopard seal, which hunts fish, and, at the ice edge, penguins; and the Ross seal, rarest in the Antarctic.

The elephant seal is huge, smelly, and ugly to human eyes.

The adult males have a grotesque trunklike nose. From a distance or in photographs, the elephant seal may exert a certain appeal. It has enormous liquid brown eyes, and the young seals and females without the nose can look like puzzled extraterrestrials—Slugs From Space. Up close they belch and roar in appalling fashion, smell horrible, and, when they molt, plumb the depths of odiousness. The seals shed hair and skin in large patches and sheets, contaminating the meltwater pools they like to wallow in.

European and American fortune seekers killed elephant seals to boil their blubber down for oil. Although each elephant seal yielded far less oil than a whale, one did not have to hunt them at sea. The elephant seals start breeding in early fall and form colonies, with enormous bulls associated with harems of females. Some colonies contain as many as 4,000 seals. In smaller groups one bull is dominant over all. Other bulls have areas of influence, and the bulls of lowest status haunt the fringes and move from one beach colony to another. The bulls battle each other for dominance, but they are protected by a blubber layer that can be 17 centimeters thick. The males are enormous, up to 4.5 meters long and weighing 3 or 4 tons, sometimes 5. The cows are much smaller, about 2.8 meters, perhaps 900 kilograms. There are now about 800,000 elephant seals in the Southern Ocean.

These seals were killed in a different fashion than the fur seals. William Phelps, the cabin boy who was left on Marion Island, describes the process:

> These animals were not difficult to kill, being very clumsy, and slow of motion. The method was to approach them in front, with a rap on the nose, to make them rise up on their flippers, then to lance them a few times through the heart: they are very full-blooded, and would sometimes be half an hour in dying, with a number of lance-holes through the heart. The blubber was taken off in wide strips from head to foot, the tongue taken out, and the carcass left for the birds, who would clean and polish the

bones in a few days: the animal would average over half a barrel of oil, some of them yielding two.[31]

They also shot the animals. Joseph Fuller, who plied the Southern Ocean for fifty years, wrote in his diaries of the killing parties he supervised:

> Arriving on our field of operation, the officers and boatsteerers commenced to kill them. The first and second mate were to do the shooting and the boatsteerers the lancing. The elephant, after being shot and killed, has to be bled. They used Winchester rifles, caliber 44. The lances are about three feet long, and they are fixed with a socket into which fits a pole about six feet in length.
>
> It takes four men to kill a good sized bull. First of all you have to get them out of the water holes. This is accomplished by driving them out with a stick. You then commence to slaughter bulls first. The reason for doing this is because the cows will remain on the beach to protect their young, but the bulls will make straight way for the water . . . Sometimes it takes as high as ten bullets to stop them and then a good spearing to kill them . . . After all of the bulls have been slaughtered, the cows are killed and also the young. Those that are small are let go free. Now comes the skinning. It takes four men to skin a bull.
>
> They commence skinning them by cutting them from the back of the head to their tail. Then the back is skinned down as far as the stomach. After skinning him, you commence to operate on the blubber. You cut through it until you come in contact with flesh—from his head to his tail, so as to separate the blubber. You have an even quantity on each side. If the elephant is fat and has nice, thick blubber, you commence at his head or tail and cut pieces large enough for a man to carry in one hand. As you cut it off you run your knife through it and it serves for grasping a hold of. After having taken all of the blubber off the back, you turn him over on his side and go through the same performance. It takes eight or ten men to turn a good sized bull over. The men stand by with poles two men to a pole. The pole is shoved through the holes already made in the blubber; two men

> can generally carry six or seven pieces. It is conveyed to the beach and from there rafted aboard to go through the process of trying or boiling out. Skinning and conveying the blubber to the ship is kept up all day.[32]

In a strange chapter in the life of the Southern Ocean, penguins were also killed and boiled down for their oil. Usually, like elephant seals, they were killed to supplement a whaler's cargo when the whaling was not satisfactory. But on Macquarie Island off Australia, the harvesting of penguins was a major enterprise. For twenty-five years, starting in 1891, a New Zealander named Joseph Hatch killed about 150,000 king and royal penguins each season, without any permanent effect on the population.

At one point in Captain Joseph Fuller's career, he was shipwrecked on Desolation Island. He spent eleven months there with twenty-two men. He wrote of his impressions of the island from the sea:

> As you stand into the land from the northward, the land looks bleak and desolate, with the tops of the mountains covered with snow. But as you draw in with the land, you will see vegetation in green patches and them green patches is wild cabbage and moss and kind of reed like grass but not a tree or bush of no kind.[33]

Fuller lost his ship in a storm. He and most of his men were already on shore, and the ship anchored some way off. After the storm had cleared he went to look for the ship and saw that it was gone:

> Only my God knows with what a sad and sorrowful heart that I returned to the tent knowing that I had twenty-two men to look after and some of them hard characters; one or two of them had not been out of prison long before we sailed from home and one of the boatsteerers was not much better, but there was some good men among them. But in going down I made up my mind that there must be a head and that I should be that head and if

any of them did not comply with my orders then some one should get hurt.[34]

They fixed up a shanty to stay in, and Fuller insisted on working with the men, sharing equally in labor and provisions. A party he sent out to scout for wreckage returned with this report: "'But Captain Fuller, the best of all; the whiskey barrel has come on shore all right and I rolled it up in the grass and before we came away we took a good swig out of it.' I told him that I could see that without he telling me of it."[35] Fuller drained the whiskey barrel out onto the sand.

The men were not desperate. They did not face Antarctic temperatures, and the land provided enough to eat. In fact, they had enough presence of mind to think of writing down what was happening. There were arguments over writing paper. Long before the age of instant celebrities, people who had experienced adventures or disasters were already keeping an eye on the possibility of publication. Fuller kept order, and he seems to have had no talent for melancholy, no great interest in meditating on his plight.

Of course, all was not hardship. He wrote of the Sunday dinner the men all took together: "I do not know that I ever eat anything as nice as young albatross. Even when it is frying the smell is most delicious. But the best of all we had good appetite for sauce and good cold water to wash it down."[36]

Two weeks after Fuller finally returned home to New London someone asked him what he would do next. "I told him I suppose I should have to go to sea again, as I had to do something for a living."[37]

The elephant sealing industry did not collapse because of a boom and bust approach. The demand was never as great as for fur seals, perhaps. The hunters seemed to kill mainly bulls, each of which would be seven times as large as a female and give much more blubber for the effort. And because of the social arrangements of elephant seals, as long as there were females to breed, there were always numerous surplus bulls ready to take the place of an older, bigger one that had been killed.

Despite the bloody nature of seal killing, the sealers were not immune to pity or perhaps even empathy for the creatures they killed. One shipwrecked sealer told of finding a cave on shore with the entrance "partially closed by what might be termed immense bars of ice, formed like icicles of gigantic magnitude, standing as pillars of crystal at the entrance of some fairy cavern!" Looking inside through this "wonderful and beautiful display of congelation" he saw not mermaids, but fourteen young sea elephants, as they were called. He broke the ice bars and set them free, with no apparent sense of the irony of his action.[38]

Speculation about the past often reveals more about the speculator than it does about history. But the sealers were different men, from a different time than Scott, Amundsen, and Shackleton—the figures of the heroic age. The battle is still being waged in the names of these heroes, as to who was the strongest, the most noble, the best. There was romance to the stories of these men; to their lives, their plans, their hopes; to the whole enterprise of exploration for the sake of exploration.

For the sealers, profit, not romance, was the dominant theme. To be sure, one could pursue fortune at home as well as on the seas; men became bankers and salesmen as well as sealers. But to the sealers and whalers the sea was much like a mine. There was gold to be found, procured, kept from competitors. In their logs they comment on their surroundings, but more often in terms of weather or difficulty than of beauty or romance. By the evidence of their journals they were not reflective men. There is little hint of whether they loved the sea, or hated it, or feared it, or felt all of these emotions. Clearly they did not "appreciate" it in the way tourists and poets now appreciate nature. In the presence of extraordinary actuality, you might say, their consciousness was sharpened and narrowed by the intensity of their desire to a particular point of attention—the finding and killing of seals. Alternatively, you could argue it was indeed their imagination that drove them, except that they imagined commerce, trade, farms, money. Their imagination made the Southern Ocean into a resource, something to be used, not meditated upon.

Their habits were rapacious, their methods brutal, but I find myself admiring them, whereas I react to the escapades of the explorers as perverse. I have never read a more distressing story than Apsley Cherry-Garrard's, *The Worst Journey in the World,* in which he describes a trek in the Antarctic winter, in temperatures of minus 70 degrees, to get eggs of emperor penguins.[39] Why didn't he and the others turn back when they saw what an absurd pursuit they were undertaking?

The sealers commended their souls to the Almighty or the devil, and took what chances they needed to. I cannot imagine they ever sought out hardship. The explorers, in contrast, spat into the wind, daring nature to take their lives. They took foolish chances. This analysis suggests, of course, that money, even perhaps a fortune, is necessary, whereas glory, personal challenges, and adventure are not. This is a notion I would never have expected myself to hold, but perhaps growing up in New England, in fact in Connecticut, from which many sealers came, had more effect on me than I ever imagined.

Chapter 4

PORT

If the Southern Ocean has a port town, it is McMurdo. The research station has been compared to a mining town or a frontier town, but there is no single description that does it justice. McMurdo's more than eighty buildings cover 200 acres of dirty snow, ice, dust, and makeshift boardwalks on Ross Island. It is an uneasy mixture of construction site, military base, and college campus. It has a population in the summer of 1,500 people, with a total of 3,000 passing through it on their way in and out of the field. The icebreaker and supply ship dock at the ice pier, which is formed of a mixture of water and gravel and cables laid throughout.

Bringing the icebreaker into the ice pier was a delicate task. The pier was new and only about 12 feet thick, exactly the sort of ice the *Polar Sea* was designed to smash. Although the operations officer must have spent a couple of hours easing into the pier, it cracked anyway. Later, during the unloading of the supply ship, the pier cracked into several pieces.

Seeing land after two weeks at sea, or perhaps "at ice," was more exhilarating than I expected. I had been told that a sure sign of being at sea too long was when McMurdo looked good. And a sure sign of being at McMurdo too long was when the *Polar Sea* looked good.

McMurdo and the surrounding area are saturated with the remnants and lore of polar expeditions. Robert Falcon Scott undertook the first in 1901 on the *Discovery*. His first landing in Antarctica was at Cape Adare on the coast of Victoria Land. He then took his ship south and after two more landings came to McMurdo Sound. Hut Point at McMurdo is named for the base where Scott's team built three huts. Scott's hut is maintained as a museum by the New Zealand Antarctic program. The hut, within easy walking distance and plain view of McMurdo's sprawl, is the focal point of the Scott's Hut Race, conducted each season. The race covers about 5 kilometers, and the T-shirts awarded to everyone who finishes are coveted enough that the race draws a huge crowd, many of them walking.

From Hut Point, Scott made his first attempt on the South Pole, with Edward Wilson and Ernest Shackleton. They made it to 82 degrees 16 minutes south, the farthest anyone had gone toward the Pole, and had to turn back. They suffered horribly from scurvy on the return but made it to Hut Point safely on February 3, 1903.

Ernest Shackleton made his own attempt on the Pole in 1908. He couldn't reach Hut Point and set up a base at Cape Royds, also on Ross Island. Shackleton got even closer to the Pole. He turned around only 180 kilometers from it, and when he returned to England he was knighted.

The final race to the Pole, between Roald Amundsen and Scott, which has been recounted over and over, took place in 1911. Amundsen set off from his base on the Ross Ice Shelf by the Bay of Whales, east of Ross Island and McMurdo, and closer to the Pole. Scott constructed his camp at Cape Evans, on Ross Island, between Hut Point, where he had made his first camp, and Cape Royds, where Shackleton had his base. The results are, of course, legend. Amundsen reached the South Pole on December 14, 1911. Scott reached it on January 18, 1912. Amundsen returned safely with all his men. Scott and the four men with him failed to make it back to their base and died on the way. Scott, however, was thought to have died gloriously, and so became the hero of the English-speaking world. Only recently has he come under attack, in particular by Roland Huntford, in his book *Scott and Amundsen: The Race to the South Pole,* which portrays Scott as indecisive and incompetent.[1] Scott's last base, at Camp Evans, is also preserved. For some years the environmental group Greenpeace maintained a base camp on the same beach.

Heavy machinery rolls throughout McMurdo, and trailers and ramshackle buildings are strewn about. But the base is also full of navy personnel, who set the tone in important ways. The cafeteria is divided into an officers' and an enlisted mess. And there are five bars segregated by rank, a bowling alley, and a place to rent skis, guitars, and other toys. And McMurdo is integrated, largely thanks to the navy. The civilian personnel and scientists, male and female, are mostly white but, since the military is arguably the most integrated institution in the United States, there are many more black people in McMurdo than at the average U.S. construction site.

Still, the tone cannot be said to be really military either. The scientists, and their graduate students, and the fellow-traveling civilian employees—many of whom are college age—give the place a campus aura. When I arrived, the first thing I did was to find a room. I checked in at the central office, known as the Chalet, and was assigned a room at a dormitorylike building called the Hotel California. On my first day at McMurdo I visited an art show, composed of work by some of the 1,500 residents. A group of women sang madrigals. A long-haired man gave what appeared to be a competent display of Balinese music. One artist, a woman, had displayed a nude self-portrait.

I had been on the icebreaker for three weeks, but it was three weeks with about 120 men and one woman. And the social norms of military life seem male even when practiced by women—the titles, the hierarchy, the joking insults. After time on the frozen sea, on a boat, preoccupied with science, the military, and fuel spills, McMurdo, which is certainly in the running for drabbest human habitation of all time, seemed like an explosion of sensuality. Madrigals. Balinese music. Women out of uniform. Bars. Soda machines filled with beer (75 cents). Art. Nude self-portraits.

The civilian workers in Antarctica come under contract. Many hope to experience the continent but end up spending most of their time working in the mess or cleaning rooms at the Hotel California. The standard joke about civilian workers is this: The first year you come for the experience. The second year you come for the money. The third year you're not fit for anything else.

It is difficult for anyone to get away from McMurdo to explore because Antarctica is so dangerous. Right outside the mundane world of mess hall and officers' club is the cold continent itself. Skiing and hiking are allowed, for instance, only on carefully marked trails. A few years before I arrived a party of three young men out for a day hike in good weather took a shortcut, off the marked and approved path. As they were walking along the man in the center looked to the left and saw his friend was gone. He looked to the right and saw that his other friend was gone. Both had just fallen into crevasses. He lay down and crawled out of danger. Both his friends were dead by the time he brought help back.

I had my own room, two beds, two desks, two sets of drawers for clothes. Roommates occasionally appeared for a night or two, passing through. The hotel was primarily for transients, although many were not as transient as they would have preferred. The weather often kept scientists who had finished their fieldwork at the hotel long past their official departure dates. In fact, the difficulty of getting out of McMurdo to fly home turned out to be the reason for the hotel's name. It was drawn from the song by The Eagles that included the verse: "You can check out any time you like, but you can never leave."

William Hammer of Augustana College in Illinois, who had just discovered some dinosaur bones in the area of the Beardmore Glacier, stayed at the hotel during my time there. Each day for at least seven days, he and several members of his group dragged their bags off to Willy Field to fly to New Zealand, and from there back to the United States. Each day I saw them dragging their bags back after the flight was canceled.

McMurdo was the opposite of the *Polar Sea* in one important way. On the ship I had gotten used to sleeping through a lot of noise in complete darkness. At the Hotel California the nights were bright and quiet. The sun shone directly in my window at 11 P.M. This was a small price to pay for much greater mobility. I was free to explore, to chase scientists down to talk to them, to hitch rides on helicopters or, if I preferred, to spend days holed up reading novels by John Updike.

I was hardly there at all as far as the National Science Foundation was concerned. This part of my trip had no agenda. I could stay with the icebreaker or at McMurdo. There was room at the hotel, so I was welcome to hang out. McMurdo is a bit like an Ivy League school—very hard to get into but easy to navigate once you're there. It took me two years of applications, proposals to the NSF, and book proposals to publishers to get the National Science Foundation to take me south.

But once in McMurdo, many things are possible for the hitchhiker on the Antarctic enterprise. Another mouth to feed at the mess is not noticeable. There are rooms at the Hotel California. Flights out are hard to arrange, but I had a return ticket on the icebreaker. I snagged rides on helicopters, airplanes, and Sprites (vehicles that are something like jeeps with tractor treads). I went to snow school. I probably could have arranged a ride to the South Pole if I could have made an argument that it was necessary for my research but, considering that I was to write about the ocean and not the continent, that seemed excessive.

So, trapped in a small research base at the very bottom of the world, I experienced an exhilarating freedom. It was Club Med in Antarctica—nothing to buy, no place to spend money, except at the bars, and no place that I had to be, nothing that I had to do, no itinerary. I achieved at McMurdo something far more difficult in the civilized world than finding real wilderness. I was bureaucratically invisible.

The first thing I did was sign up for snow school, to learn elementary techniques of survival. At the preparatory meeting the positive attitude was as thick as the scorn and pessimism would be in a graduate school literature seminar. The instructors told us not to let other people do the tasks we were about to learn: lighting a stove, packing a survival bag. We had to take responsibility for our own learning, to participate, to be alive and aware. It was the Church of Outward Bound.

The outdoor instructors/ministers had self-confidence that glowed like an ozone-hole sunburn, and they liked others who had it as well. They had no time for complainers. They liked doers. Irony was not only not appreciated, it was not noticed. I began to think that perhaps I was on the wrong continent.

When I was young, before I was a fan of Phil Ochs and sang "I Declare the War Is Over" and "White Boots Marching in a Yellow Land" out my dorm room window on football weekends, my fondest wish was to be a marine like my father. I reveled in his stories of how tough the drill instructors were at Parris Island. I too was going to meet the challenge and prove I was worthy. I was going to show that I could duckwalk around the parade ground and clean the latrine with a toothbrush if I had to. Militarism soured for most people of my generation. But the old soldierly yearning for the drill instructor experience doesn't die, it just takes on a new form. The outdoor instructor is the New Age DI. No guns, no violence, and no goldbricking—call it the War on Whining.

Field training began on a balmy day (in the 40s and sunny enough to give skin cancer to a seal) with cooperative games. First we all sat on each other's knees to form a daisy chain, interlocked, interdependent circle. Then the instructors instructed us on hypothermia and frostbite. Then we built our snow shelter. We cut blocks of snow to build our group's kitchen. We set up the tents. We built a wall to block the wind.

By some stroke of luck, two extremely large men were part of our group: one from Minnesota and one from Georgia. Both were civilians and both were in the workingman mold, not wandering college boys. The Georgian had just gotten out of the army and when he talked over the radio to our leaders, he produced a completely believable military chatter, with much Alpha, Bravo, Charlie talk. The two men hewed and heaved snow as if they were constructing Valhalla. I felt that perhaps a higher power was looking out for me. By chance I had landed Fasolt and Fafner as partners.

The snow dome that we built was the sort that you make if you are stranded, perhaps in an emergency landing of a ski plane or helicopter, with all your gear and bags. You have food, you have sleeping bags and tents, you are not in immediate danger. But the weather in Antarctica, even on the mild coast, can go from 30 degrees to minus 30 degrees overnight, with blowing snow and wind added for emphasis. So shelter is of the utmost importance. Tents are okay; snow shelters are better.

First we piled all our bags in a dome shape. Then we cut and packed snow all over the bags until we had created a dome with 2-foot thick walls. Then, to get in and get the bags out, we dug down in the snow outside the shelter, tunneled underneath and up into the shelter. We dragged the bags out through this tunnel. The design was extremely effective; the tunnel served as a trap for cold air, and the dome stayed warm and cozy.

I myself had staked out a tent. I have mild claustrophobia and the way I saw it, there was a serious flaw in our design. The tunnel was so long and small that you had to crawl through on your belly, like a reptile. I am about 6 feet tall, or long, when I am flat on my stomach in a tiny tunnel with no room to move, and when I was in mid-crawl I was entirely enclosed by the tunnel, my feet well past the entrance, my head not yet into the dome. The interior of the dome was also pretty small. It was supposed to have room for four people or so. It had room for two. And there was no quick way to get out. I decided that a tent was the better part of valor.

Fafner, from Minnesota, was the only one sleeping in the dome. In our group there were two tents. I had one and Fasolt had nailed the other. There was no way he was crawling into the dome and getting stuck in there. But that left Freia, who had smuggled some alcohol along on this outing (the civilian workers, like me, considered snow school a kind of vacation). Alcohol was forbidden on this trip because it can lead to dehydration and hypothermia. She was planning to sleep in Fasolt's tent, but then he turned in early and started snoring. That was the complaint of record, at any rate. She too had claustrophobia and feared the dome. So there we were, four of us, Fasolt already snoring, Fafner in the dome, Freia on the verge of tears, and me.

I did the right thing and gave my tent to Freia. I didn't want to return home and have to tell my children that I gave up my one chance in life to sleep in a snow dome in Antarctica because I was chicken and made someone even more distressed than I was go through the long dark tunnel. So I crawled into the dome and found room for my sleeping bag on one side of the small interior. Fafner and I discussed what to do with the gear we'd brought inside. He wanted to pile it all up to

The U.S. Coast Guard cutter *Polar Sea*, moored in the ice on its way from Australia to Antarctica to open up an ice-free passage to McMurdo Research Station.

Cape Horn, where the southernmost tip of South America reaches into the Southern Ocean.

ABOVE LEFT: Chunks of broken ice the size of small automobiles pass along the starboard side of the *Polar Sea* on their way aft to be milled by the ship's screws.
ABOVE RIGHT: The wake of the *Polar Sea*: The icebreaker leaves a path of crumbled ice that freezes over again.

Sea ice: In the austral winter, twenty million square kilometers of the Southern Ocean's surface freeze over.

Tabular iceberg: These flat mesas of ice break off from the ice shelves that rim Antarctica.

Fur seals on Elephant Island: These seals, now flourishing, were hunted almost to extinction in a commercial rush during the late eighteenth and early nineteenth centuries.

Elephant seals: Enormous and malodorous, these creatures were once killed for the oil that their blubber yields.

McMurdo Research Station, Ross Island, Antarctica, as seen from McMurdo Sound. (Photograph courtesy of Stanley S. Jacobs)

The Dry Valleys: These rare ice-free regions can have an otherworldly calm in summer, but in winter merciless winds whip the landscape.

A view of ramshackle McMurdo in the late 1970s: It gets cleaner every year. (Photograph courtesy of Stanley S. Jacobs)

Whale bones and tourists on Deception Island: Early-twentieth-century Antarctic whalers butchered whales over the side in Deception's protected harbor. They then set the carcasses adrift to wash ashore and rot.

King penguins nesting on South Georgia: The males and females take turns holding the egg on their feet. A flap of loose skin folds over the egg to keep it warm.

Ventifacts—huge boulders and small stones carved by the wind—are sometimes reminiscent of abstract sculptures.

ABOVE LEFT: Mating dance: After years without touching land, young wandering albatrosses have returned to South Georgia to find a mate. Here two birds are in the midst of courtship. ABOVE RIGHT: Chinstrap penguin: These birds live in colonies of tens of thousands on the islands just off the Antarctic Peninsula.

Rusted and abandoned, a whale catcher, its harpoon gun still on the bow, lies in the harbor at Grytviken, South Georgia. Whaling from the island stopped in the 1960s.

Tourists cruise in an inflatable boat among icebergs off the Antarctic Peninsula.

block the entrance to the tunnel, thereby keeping us really warm. Even though Fafner was huge, and the snow walls of the dome were such that I thought I could punch through them if I had to, I vetoed this option on the grounds that we had to have enough air to last the night.

Naturally, the snow shelter was perfect. Despite melting ice dripping on my neck a bit during the night, it was warm and quiet and smelled fresh and clean. When we went to sleep it was probably about 35 degrees outside, with clear skies and very little wind. I assumed it was the same when I woke up. But after I got dressed and wriggled outside, the sun was gone, the wind was blowing, there was snow in the air, and the temperature had dropped 15 or 20 degrees.

McMurdo is run, officially, by the National Science Foundation. The navy has its role, but the theory, and to a large extent the reality, is that the Antarctic is run by and for scientists. In the lingo of McMurdo, the scientists are "beakers." The Antarctic is rife with the nicknames and initials and inside talk that any isolated group develops. For instance, the South Pole is called "Pole." If you talk about going to *the* South Pole, or *the* Pole, you are clearly not in the club. One flies to Pole, plain and simple. One spends time at Pole. One has been or has not been to Pole. If you say it wrong you are clearly not an OAE—Old Antarctic Explorer.

Anyone who spends enough time on the ice risks death by acronym. There are DVs (distinguished visitors), and GFAs (general field assistants or something less polite), and there is NGA (nongovernmental activity). Greenpeace and anyone associated with them is NGA, sometimes used as a noun. There are U-barrels (urine barrels for recycling of human waste). And then there are the acronyms that are jokes about acronyms: CBA, Continent of Baffling Acronyms, and HEKTMOTFOTE, a favorite of everyone's—Harshest Environment Known to Man on the Face of the Earth. Not to forget the Safety Health Implementation

Teams described by one investigator as SHITs. Sometimes the Antarctic experience feels like being trapped in a computer lab with a bunch of adolescents who've had too much coffee.

One paradoxical aspect of the elusiveness of the ocean is that its shores are among the best places to look for its identity and nature. McMurdo has the greatest concentration of scientists in one place studying the Southern Ocean. It also has a dive operation.

I made it a point to seek out the dive master, Jim Herpolsheimer. He was trim, fit, thoughtful, and precise in conversation; a writer of poetry, short stories, and screenplays. He was also, like all the technophiles and scientists and field operators in the Antarctic, like all the Coasties, a practicing optimist, self-reliant and confident. He displayed the kind of self-confidence you see time and again in pilots, sky divers, climbers, and of course outdoor instructors.

Herpolsheimer had been down to Mactown, as McMurdo is often called, four times, twice wintering over for fourteen-month stretches. In one of those stretches he learned French, learned how to tap dance, and taught himself to write fiction. He had published some of his short stories and, when I talked to him, he was working on screenplays and scripts for television. His attitude toward writing was similar to his attitude toward the challenges of diving in the Antarctic. With regard to making a living as a writer, he said: "It can be done. And if it can be done, I can do it."

He had been diving since 1968, but this was his first year running the dive locker. The most significant fact about diving in the Antarctic, he said, was not the safety measures required for ice diving, which apply in other extremely cold seas, but the clarity of the water. The Antarctic waters are the clearest seas on earth.

When the waters are clearest, early in the summer season before the plankton bloom is going full blast, the visibility is over 400 feet, Herpolsheimer estimated. Divers in Long Island Sound are ecstatic to have 20 feet visibility. In the Caribbean, 80 to 100 feet is considered lovely. After the Antarctic, according to Herpolsheimer, "Everywhere else in the world you're diving in a cloud."

Under the ice, one is weightless, in a still world, flying. The ice cover keeps the surface of the water perfectly calm. Underneath the surface, very little moves. There is plenty of fish life but it doesn't move much. Only once had Herpolsheimer seen fish moving in the water column. Usually they sit on the bottom.

"There's a feeling, particularly in the early season. I'm tempted to be hyperbolic and say it's like diving in a cathedral. The space, the quiet, the ceiling above, the quick dropoff into darkness—here when you dive you know there's nothing to hurt you. But one has the feeling of intruding on the giants' domain, like Grieg's Hall of the Mountain King.

"The most spectacular dive I ever made in my life was down here. At Hutton Cliffs. There is multiyear ice here 17 to 20 feet thick and pressure ridges that rise up and go down. It was a huge, jumbled array of ice which had opened up to make a crack. We got in near the cliff. Sixty feet down we swam through this array of broken ice. Seals swam by while we were going through the ice, almost close enough to touch. Then you're in an area where there's no bottom, blue water, and the crack and pressure ridge above. It was like floating in space, with seals everywhere around you." These were Weddell seals, the deepest divers among sea mammals other than whales.

Not all the Antarctic seals inspire the same feelings of awe and pleasure. Nobody much likes leopard seals, which lurk by the ice edge to catch Adelie penguins. But they do respect them. Earlier that season a young student research assistant had been bitten by a leopard seal. She was collecting water samples at the ice edge. The seal leaped out of the water, closed its jaws around the young woman's knee, and then, apparently realizing that she was not a penguin, let go. The bite did not break the skin, but the seal, before it recognized its mistake, had closed its jaws strongly enough to leave a clear imprint. The bite mark was matched against the jaws of what was considered a large leopard seal skull in the biology building. The seal that had bitten the young woman was larger than the specimen.

A few days after my talk with Herpolsheimer I went along with him to help out on a dive. We flew to Cape Evans with Larry Basch, who was working with a group from the University of California at Santa Cruz studying invertebrates, and a couple of other helpers. It was a warm, sunny day, in the 30s, and we were dressed, as required for all helicopter flights, in full Antarctic regalia—long underwear, parkas, heavy pants—in case we got stranded. You can always take clothes off. You can't put on what you don't have.

We landed on the ice within view of one of Scott's huts, from his 1910–13 expedition, at a hole that the scientists and divers had been keeping open. First we set up anchors in the ice around it. Then the divers put on their gear. The "dressing in" was a lot like getting ready for a space walk. The temperature of the water, which stays pretty even year round, was about 29 degrees. The balmy weather made it easier to get undressed and put on the proper outfit, but it also increased the danger of overheating.

The first layer Basch and Herpolsheimer put on was expedition-weight Capilene underwear. In the air, at 29 degrees, doing any kind of movement, this layer itself, combined with a windbreaker, would be too much. Over this they put on a Thinsulate suit, the thin, high-tech equivalent of a full-body down parka. Next came the dry suit. A wet suit lets in water, which is warmed by your body and forms an insulating layer. Below about 55 degrees the water is too cold for the body to warm. Dry suits, which seal the body off from the water, are necessary.

The cuffs, hand and feet, and the neck seal are of critical importance, and very unpleasant for the diver who is dressing in, particularly the neck seal. Imagine the struggle of getting a too-tight turtleneck over the face of a two-year old, then imagine that the turtleneck is made of neoprene or latex. The seal is part of a hood that tightly encases the head, leaving only parts of the face unprotected. At one point before the divers entered the water, as they were struggling with neck and wrist seals, gloves and hoods, Larry Basch looked as if he was going to faint from the heat. He was completely sealed and insulated. The sun was out. The air temperature was warming up. He was being poached in his own juices. By the time he got in the water, the cold was a relief.

The divers stayed under for a full hour. At one point a Coast Guard helicopter touched down nearby, the Antarctic version of stopping by the neighbor's to chat. The talk turned to Greenpeace, which had its camp on shore, within sight. When we had just landed, before the dive began, the skuas, like large gulls, were hanging out around our gear and food, pecking at it. I had picked up an ice chunk to shy at them, and Herpolsheimer had warned me not to do it, not with Greenpeace right there. He was quite serious.

Because of past conflicts with Greenpeace and criticism of NSF's environmental record, many of them valid, environmental correctness was on everybody's mind. I was amazed. I had no hope of hitting the bird. Skuas are not in the least endangered. And I know in my bones that my ancestors back to *Australopithecus* on the African veldt threw objects at scavenging birds to keep them away from primate food. It is part of the natural order.

Human waste was another matter of deep concern. All human waste is supposed to be recycled in sensitive environments in Antarctica. There was some confusion as to whether peeing on the ice was forbidden. The scientists I talked to described it as NGA. It seemed to me, and certainly to many of them, that a world in which people worry about pissing on the ice is a poorer one. In the interests of full disclosure I will confess right here. Let Greenpeace and the NSF and the EDF and the NRDC come and seek me out and make an example of me. I am guilty. More than once I pissed on the ice. So far there are no rules about farting below the Antarctic Circle.

I never saw it written down, but the understanding was that we were not supposed to visit Greenpeace, much less bring them treats from the McMurdo mess. Greenpeace was the ne plus ultra of NGA. And, naturally, most of the civilian support personnel were big fans of Greenpeace. In the class structure of the Antarctic, the civilian workers were the proletariat—they worked for the beakers, got bossed around by the navy, and had the least freedom.

An English television crew that had come with Greenpeace arrived at McMurdo one day while I was there. According to the Antarctic Treaty, the international agreement that governs the activities of the many nations active on and around the continent, nobody owns the land in Antarctica. But you can own the buildings. Journalists like myself, brought down under NSF auspices, have the run of the station. There was never any attempt that I could discern to keep me or anyone in my position from talking to anyone, from seeing anything. There were and are no restrictions on what I write. If I decided after my trip to trash the NSF, so be it. But if you go down with Greenpeace the reception is a good deal chillier. These unofficial reporters were not allowed in the NSF buildings unless invited in by a scientist. Most of the scientists were busy.

There is a reason for this attitude beyond the natural antagonism between government and activists. Greenpeace had put out the word a few years before that McMurdo Sound was as polluted as Boston Harbor. The NSF has never forgiven them for that, or forgotten. It was actually a much smaller area that was, indeed, horrendously polluted, not the whole sound.

The NSF has spent millions to clean up McMurdo, and is still spending, as well as vigorously enforcing strict rules on recycling and waste management. But even bureaucrats and the occasional researchers who bitterly resent Greenpeace's attitude toward facts will admit that without that group's gadfly efforts in the field, combined with the legal efforts of the Environmental Defense Fund in Washington, the cleanup of McMurdo would have been a lot slower.

When the divers came up, overheating was no longer a problem. They had been down 60 feet on a rolling gravel bottom with rock outcrops. There were red algae on the bottom, sea urchins all over, small fish, sea stars, ribbon worms. The worms secrete a slimy mucus. Once it gets on a dive suit it smells forever. Basch and Herpolsheimer had collected urchins and sea stars for Basch's research. There were also soft corals, anemones, and hydroids. But there was minimal color. The light is filtered by the ice, and depending on visibility and the thickness of the ice the color underwater runs from light blue to gray.

After the divers escaped from the suits, we all walked over the ice to visit Scott's hut. This had been his base during the fatal 1911 assault on the Pole. He reached the goal second, after Roald Amundsen had been there, and died with four of his men on the way back. We walked in and around the hut, looking at old bridles, a dead seal, seal blubber stacked in layers like a grotesque cake and melting a bit at the bottom. Inside the hut the tins and utensils and notes were in no apparent order. The New Zealand Antarctic Program was in the process of doing an inventory, and some of the items had been moved. The bunks were short. Cans of Wellington's Pea Flour and Scotch Kale and tins of spices rested unopened on shelves and tables. Skis were leaning against the walls. On one table lay the carcass of a small emperor penguin.

From there we walked a few hundred yards to the Greenpeace camp. The camp looked cozy, with books and a television for videos. The men and women we stopped in to see were still tidying up from a big party for all the summer folk who went back on the Greenpeace ship *Gondwana*. Just as we were beginning to talk, and they were getting tea and cookies ready for us, our helicopter arrived.

There is no question about NSF's attempt to clean up its act. In addition to making navy helicopter pilots carry out containers of human waste, and not even navy waste, a task that the pilots were not fond of, the NSF has developed recycling and waste management plans and closed the dump that used to spill everything from jeeps to fuel barrels into the bay.

To figure out just how things were in the bay, the NSF also contracted with a group from Moss Landing Marine Laboratories in California to look at the bay and see how badly disturbed it was. While I was in McMurdo, John Oliver from Moss Laboratories, who was heading up the field team, gave a talk. In the north, he said, gray whales stir up the sea bottom, making huge holes, and walruses blow away sediment looking for food, scarring the bottom as well. Icebergs gouge roads into the sea floor. After them come scavengers, invertebrates that Oliver compares to jackals. "Here these are amphipods. They're small and voracious, most of them less than an inch long. They'll eat a cod as it's being pulled up, starting at the tail. When you're diving, they'll start to eat your lips."

What Oliver found on the sea floor in the sound was anchor ice, growing there, then floating up, ripping up the sea bottom. He also found abundant life, forests of sponges, worms, starfish, and all sorts of other creatures. "The bottom is covered with living things. We find valleys of sponges 1,000 years old ripped up by anchor ice."

The biggest disturbance he found was in Winter Quarters Bay, and was caused by what fell in from the old dump. "The damage from the dump is mostly contained in a backwater. In this area the 55-gallon drum is ubiquitous. There are also cargo containers. In Barrel Valley, about 30 percent coverage by barrels . . . there is a fuselage of a DC-3." That wasn't all. There was Mactown sewage as well. He reported that divers could see a cloud in the water, almost a wall of particulates, at times of day when a lot of people were flushing toilets.

There was still life in the bay, but the sediment was saturated with oily material. An analysis showed that it had been burned before it got there, and Oliver concluded that the material probably came from ships' bilges. Even in the bay, however, conditions have improved. There are many more fish than there had been in the 1970s or 1980s.

Oliver concluded that the bay was "as bad as some of our worst harbors" in the United States. But, he said, "you could hit a baseball out of it. Some of the neatest bottom communities in Antarctica are just a hop, skip, and a jump away."

By way of introduction, Oliver had also offered an insight into the peculiar freewheeling nature of McMurdo, within the limits of the constant and often exhausting scientific work. He talked about applying for a grant as coming up with "the Excuse" to "play the Game," which is always related to the excuse, but never exactly the same. Scientists cast their research proposals in terms that fit the needs and interests of the granting agency as they understand them. So they may be doing work on pollution. But they may also be interested in all disturbances of the ocean floor, in the Antarctic itself, in the process of understanding an extreme environment. They may be Edwardian explorers manqué.

It struck me that my situation in McMurdo was much the same. My excuse was to find out as much as I could about the Southern Ocean. Once down in Antarctica, however, the game was to see and do whatever I could, to travel to the dry valleys, to fly in helicopters, even to spend time holed up in my room reading. The game had to fit within the parameters of the excuse, but it was, fundamentally, play.

Chapter 5

LARVAL SHAPES

If you don't love invertebrates, marine biology in Antarctica is a limited field. McMurdo was my introduction to invertebrates. My previous interest had been in penguins, seals, whales—the fuzzy, furry, or at least warm-blooded creatures that are somewhat closely related to me. I had eaten clams, but I had never appreciated them, much less the larvae of starfish and sea urchins.

I first realized that some people experienced feelings about invertebrates that I did not when I was sitting in the lounge of the biology building, a hallway with a few chairs and a place to make hot cocoa. The biology building was run by several women who called themselves the "bio-blondes." There was a sign on the office that said "Blondes Only." It was a comfortable place, a welcome respite from the navy mess, and most of the scientists whose work I was interested in were attached to this lab, so I spent a lot of time there.

This particular evening Larry Basch, one of the divers I

accompanied on the diving trip at Cape Evans, was talking to one of Oliver's divers about a scale worm, a creature that usually grows to an inch or so. The diver, who had the physique and the aura of a football player or wrestler, had seen one about a foot long. He had taken a picture of the creature, which looked more like a giant louse than a worm. Basch narrowed the thing's taxonomy down to the level of family, but he couldn't make the identification any more exact. He told the diver that although he was not a big fan of "offing" creatures just for the purposes of taxonomy, he would have done it in this case, because it might have been quite a find. The diver replied: "I wasn't prepared to do anything like that. It was too magnificent an animal."

The comment took me by surprise. I found it hard to understand reverence toward an organism that was not only as ugly, by my standards, as a slug, but probably not conscious in any way we can imagine. Magnificent, he called it. I realized then that there were realms of sympathy and appreciation of the world that I had not yet begun to explore. It was an epiphany of sorts, one that marked the first step on the road to invertebrate devotion. And Basch, an invertebrate biologist, was my guide.

Basch's particular interest was in sea stars. He was working on a species that has a close cousin on the California coast, near Monterey. Naturally, in the different environments they have different rates of development—the ones in warm water grow faster than the ones in cold water. But the difference is not temperature. In one experiment Basch provided unlimited food to a slow-developing Antarctic species. Development that usually took three months took three weeks instead, closer to the Monterey timetable. In Monterey there is food all year round. In McMurdo the peak of food availability lasts only about 10 percent of the year.

Basch took me down to the aquarium. It is a typical McMurdo building, looking a bit like a shed. And it was full of tubs and tanks all fed with seawater from the sound, with tables and shelves cluttered with microscopes and petri dishes.

A new biology building was being built at the time, carefully designed to provide modern laboratory space. This was part of an ongoing attempt to make McMurdo into an environmentally sound outpost in the last wilderness, devoted to understanding the world, not trashing it. But whatever is gained by new designs—efficiency, a lessening of the impact on the environment, perhaps even some aesthetic satisfaction in the buildings themselves—something will be lost. In an odd way, it will be the impression of wildness.

Everything at McMurdo when I was there suggested, paradoxically, the power of nature. The ramshackle buildings, the unplanned sprawl, even the unregulated dumping announced that this was not our place, that we were barely making it. The sense was that the Antarctic was so powerful, so overwhelming that we couldn't possibly hurt it. We had to concentrate, instead, on our own survival, on getting up some shelter quickly, on getting the work done and getting out. The managers of McMurdo had heedlessly let oil barrels and trucks and everything else slide into Winter Quarters Bay. I tried to imagine what produced this kind of carelessness, so characteristic of human beings in all of their first encounters with wilderness. A distaste for wildness? Malevolence? More likely, I thought, people tend to be careless with their garbage when they envision themselves as fragile, with limited power, and nature as inexhaustible and beyond our power to harm.

If that is so, and if recognizing the fragility of the Antarctic and learning to cart out our shit and urine marks a kind of growing up, a recognition that we seem to be in charge after all, then it also comes with the kind of sadness that always attends adulthood. It is depressingly within our power to harm this spectacular, immense, unworldly mass of ice, and we better grow up and stop acting like children.

You could call this *The End of Nature*, the title Bill McKibben gave to his book describing the ubiquity of humanity's influence on the natural world. It is true enough that a certain idea of the world, of who we are and what wildness is, has died—a romantic idea that arose late in humanity's transit from hunting and gathering to icebreaking and power-plant building. Or you could call it *Childhood's End,* after a science fiction novel by Arthur C. Clarke that is about a rite of passage for humanity as a whole.

Of course, a better designed McMurdo, with efficient waste management and amenities like summer greenhouses, for instance, while lessening the sense of the ice's authority, would also diminish the painful biophilic yearning that has to affect anyone who spends much time there. When I was visiting the aquarium, I had only been gone a month and a half from the world of loved ones and lovemaking (not to suggest that Mactown is a monastery; this refers to my experience only) and children and plants and pets and gardens. And yet I had already been weighed down by the ice and the military and the Hotel California.

I started out knowing that the ocean was as fecund as it was cold, somehow as much a source of life as a warm sea over a coral reef. But on the icebreaker I had been wrapped in a machine. And at McMurdo, as I pursued biologists, we talked in the abstract, of indirect and direct developers, of offspring, of evolution. The analytic structure of science seemed to distance me as effectively from the life of the ocean as had the thick hull of the *Polar Sea.*

And now, down in the dreary aquarium, I looked, at Basch's request, through the dissecting microscope to see the shape of the larvae themselves. The forbidding cold, the rule-bound military environment, the NSF bureaucracy faded in the face of these living origami, translucent folds of living tissue. They were, I was compelled to imagine—with their delicate invaginations—feminine. I had been reading John Updike in my spare time, and in the absence of physical intimacy and affection his extraordinarily intimate physical descriptions of women filled my thoughts.[1] Perhaps in consequence these infoldings, these flowerings before me under the microscope struck me as nothing so much as impressionist renderings of vulvae. The resemblance was not clinical or explicit, more like Georgia O'Keeffe's flowers than the gynecological visions of modern pornography.

But I felt that in the cold aquarium looking at microscopic forms of life I had come close to the fecund ocean, touched its secrets in some subtle and elegant way. It was as if the great macroscopic movements of its whales and seals and penguins and albatrosses were so much disposable posturing—male, expendable, noisy and vulgar, a carnival for the tourists. This glimpse of starfish larvae was the voyeur's vision of the ocean's secret heart.

A scientist would object, of course, as would a bird-watcher, or a whale-watcher, not to mention a fisherman or a sailor. There is, of course, no one heart to the Southern Ocean. In geography, in time, in the interests of the people who sail and study it, the ocean is infinitely divisible, infinitely interpretable. But it would not pay to slight the small in favor of the large. There is at least as much, probably more, to be known about the ocean through invertebrates than through any other life-form.

The scientists who study invertebrates, reverential divers aside, are not, by and large, driven by an innate love for the creatures themselves. Donal Manahan, of the University of Southern California, was a perfect example. He also studied starfish and their development. I was at McMurdo while Manahan was there as a principal investigator, a PI, the highest rank available to beakers in the McMurdo social structure. He made his position clear: "We don't care about the starfish, per se." It was useful because it was a well-studied organism, common all over the world, with established baselines for its rates of development. It was also very important in the Antarctic marine world and consequently an excellent way to look at problems in development in cold seas.

The Antarctic species of starfish he was studying uses far

less energy in its development than a similar temperate one. How it does this is mysterious. Manahan fed the starfish larvae, watched their development, and tried to see what the different larvae were doing in different temperatures with different amounts of food. "The work is a bit like going to the health farm. They know what they feed you and they weigh you. If you're not losing enough weight they know you're ordering in pizza. With these guys we haven't found the pizzeria yet."

The larvae seem to be doing it by having a smaller engine, so to speak, a metabolism that putters along and is designed to use small amounts of energy efficiently. For his polar critters, giving them all they wanted to eat did not speed up development, as it did with the temperate ones. "These guys are not equipped to cope with abundance. They're programmed to work in polar environment."

Manahan got into his field partly because of his interest in the adventure of diving. He loved the sea and the activity. But in graduate school, he says, "I got the idea that the name of the game was intellectual discovery, that nobody serious gave a rat's ass what the conditions were where you collected your sample, whether you braved cold or storms. They wanted to know what you found out, how significant your scientific work was." That changed his attitude toward the sea. He had been in Belize recently, he said, which is known for having some of the world's best diving. But he didn't dive. He was "slaving away in a sweaty little room trying to get a respirometer to work."

As any scientist worth his salt would be. This is how science works. Investigators who find things out, who prosper in the conquest of knowledge and in their path through the scientific hierarchy, are predators of a sort, not unlike the early sealers and whalers and fishermen. If the sealers had a single-minded interest in getting pelts, scientists have a single-minded interest in their data. And of course, when you choose one thing, you miss others. When you do one thing seriously, thoroughly, this dedication narrows your knowledge as well as deepens it.

* * *

By the beginning of February the ice was out, and the skies were sunny. There was open water for about a mile out from the shore, a deep, satisfying blue, and many people reported seeing killer whales. I saw a minke whale coming to the surface in a slow porpoising motion. I don't know whether whales do indeed swim slowly when they are at their leisure, or if it is just their size that makes it seem as if they are moving in slow motion.

As I waited to get back on the icebreaker I felt a bit like a penguin that had been ashore too long, except that I had not been mating. I was anxious to go to sea again. A Russian ship, the *Professor Zubov*, had docked at the ice pier, and Martin Jeffries, the glaciologist, and I went onboard. It was a rust bucket with dirty wooden weather decks. The men onboard seemed to fit the ship. Perhaps they were short on water, or fuel to heat it, but the contrast between them and the scrubbed Coast Guard officers I was used to was the first thing I noticed.

As soon as we boarded the ship, crew members beckoned us to come below decks. One room was full of winter clothes. They offered us boots, anoraks, pants, coats, leather coats and pants, hats. Nothing seemed of very good quality. They had caviar, heavy wool underwear for diving (no Capilene and Thinsulate). Everyone was smoking cigarettes.

The night after the visit was Saturday. The officers' club was still open, although it was to close down for offloading of the cargo ship, the *Green Wave*, the major event of the year. All liquor sales stop for offloading. The community goes dry for however long it takes, working twenty-four hours a day to unload the ship. The idea behind this temporary prohibition is that offloading is too dangerous a time to be impaired. A lot of heavy machinery is in use, and everyone is moving and carrying heavy loads.

The officers' club was enormously crowded, and some of the

women were wearing dresses, which was a shock. They had come from a party for the Russians at the Chalet, where the NSF offices were. The Russian ship had come to McMurdo because as the Soviet Union collapsed Russia was having trouble getting people to and from its bases. The Americans were flying Russian scientists to Vostok and bringing others back. Vostok is in East Antarctica, and it is the place where the coldest temperature on earth has been recorded: minus 129.9 degrees, without the windchill. At the bar some of the Russians were steady and congenial, and others were drunk and unhappy.

One was dancing with an extremely attractive young woman, the partner of one of the navy officers. When the dance ended and she headed for the ladies' room, he came lurching by, eyes alight. He plowed through the crowd and grabbed her by the arm. He insisted that she come with him. She finally convinced him that she was going to the ladies' room. And a bit later she left the bar quietly when he wasn't looking.

The next day the story around McMurdo was that one Russian man, not necessarily the one I had watched, but perhaps in a similar spirit, had been wandering around going into rooms looking for women. Chuck Stearns, the meteorologist, confirmed that someone walked into his dorm room, went over to his bed, looked at him, and walked out. This would make the looking-for-a-woman story plausible. Any man looking for a pretty young woman could not have had a bigger disappointment. Stearns has the weathered face of an old country doctor.

Someone also walked into the room of Donal Manahan's postgraduate research assistant, John Welborn. He picked up some laundry and a fishing tackle box and walked out. Welborn followed him, keeping him in sight as he went through the dormitory, trying all the doors. The Russian walked into a couple's room and pointed at the woman. Welborn and the other American man managed to get him out of that room. Eventually Russian friends of the wanderer tried to get him to come with them, without success. Sometime that night, under unclear circumstances, he got pretty well beat up.

I was nearing the end of my stay by the time I went to observe Martin Jeffries and Willie Weeks at work in the cold room. The conditions were terrible, about 10 degrees, not counting the windchill produced by a fan. They were dressed in all their cold-weather gear, the bulky stuff they never wore out on the ice: mukluks, parkas, many-pockets pants with liners. Martin still had a bad cough, and all I could think of was a modern opera in which scientists working in a refrigerator take the place of poets in a garret.

The reason for working in such miserable circumstances was that they were dealing with ice. They were photographing slices of ice with cross polarization to get a good view of the crystalline structure. They mounted slices several inches thick on a slide with drops of water. The ice froze to the slide. Then they cut the slice down to about an eighth of an inch thickness with a table saw. Martin then worked on the slide with a sledge microtone, a hand tool that cost about $4,000. With the microtone Martin scraped the ice until the surface was flat, almost polished, with no saw marks visible. The optical filters that produce cross polarization help them produce photographs that would display the internal structure of the ice slice.

I spent a great deal of time reading—Mary Gordon, Tony Hillerman, John Barth, Updike. I watched Spalding Gray's monologue, *Swimming to Cambodia.* Actuality can only stay extraordinary for a while. Sooner or later imagination reasserts its power. Updike's adulterous pairs became as real to me as Mount Erebus. I remembered that someone said that when he was young he couldn't understand how people could spend time reading. Life was the thing. Then, older, having experienced life, he came to the conclusion that, on the whole, he preferred reading. I knew how he felt, but not why exactly. Life should have been the thing. I should have stayed awake for a month, making every attempt to drink deep of the Antarctic experience. But melancholy would overtake me, and I would retire to the Hotel California with a stack of books. Maybe it was the pull of the imagination, or maybe it was the growing dreariness of Mactown. I thought of Joyce Carol Oates's essay "Against Nature." And in an Updike short story I found a line uttered by one of the characters that expressed another idea, one contradicting the primacy of imagination in the broadest sense: "Plato was wrong: what is is absolute. Ideas pale."[2]

Updike's character said it about a woman, but it could be about the Southern Ocean, albatrosses, whales, almost anything. And it could be wrong. Spalding Gray's Cambodia was a very particular one. What, if not ideas of glory, heroism, and the nobility of the search for the unknown, had driven Scott and Amundsen? What, if not ideas, gave Scott, the man whom reality crushed and killed, a heroic immortality?

I took two trips out of McMurdo toward the center of the Antarctic continent, away from marine influence. One was a flight in a Twin Otter to check some weather stations with Stearns, the meteorologist from Wisconsin. Stearns had been to Antarctica any number of times to set up and monitor his weather stations. He took me under his wing in McMurdo. He brought me out on the Ross Ice Shelf in a tracked vehicle called a Sprite, a cross between a pickup truck and a tank. We flew to another site in a helicopter. But the memorable trip was in a Twin Otter ski plane.

Temperatures in and around McMurdo in January were seldom worse than a New York (city) winter. This was high summer, after all, and close to the moderating influence of the sea. The Reeves Glacier, where we were headed, was a bit colder, but still not worse than a New York (state) winter. One trip was canceled because it was too cold at the site to work effectively unscrewing bolts and checking equipment: 0 degrees with wind at 15 to 20 knots.

When we did fly out a couple of days later we drove a Sprite out to Willy Field a few miles away at New Zealand's Scott Base. Willy Field is an ice runway. Big, ski-equipped navy C-130 cargo planes, or Hercs, fly in and out of it, bringing cargo and people to and from New Zealand. We drove out to it past Scott Base, the New Zealand Antarctic base, only a few miles from McMurdo. On the ice in front of Scott Base, visible from the hill above it, there must have been one hundred seals looking like so many mouse turds on white counter paper.

Civilian and military flights in Antarctica are two completely different experiences. Nearly a third of the crew of the *Polar Sea* needed to be mobilized to stand by in safety positions when a helicopter was scheduled to take off or land. The number of formal checking procedures before takeoff seemed more suited to a space shot than a helicopter flight. Similarly with navy helicopter flights out of McMurdo. Safety precautions were numerous and rigid.

The Twin Otter was something else—two guys and their airplane. They were Canadians, bush pilots in the Arctic, used to flying into remote places all over the world and as informal as the military was rigid. We got in the plane, strapped ourselves in, and took off. There were only a few seats, and in the middle of what would otherwise have been the passenger cabin were two big 50-gallon drums of fuel with hoses coming out of them. During the flight the copilot would come back and switch hoses from one to the other, pumping up one of the barrels much the way you might pump up an external gasoline tank for an outboard motor on a small boat.

Stearns told me later that on an earlier flight fuel had been spitting out of one of the two engines and splattering the door of the plane. The pilots had said not to worry. Later, after refueling, the copilot apparently forgot to attach one of the hoses properly, and fuel started spurting out over the cabin. Stearns tried to tell the two pilots in the cabin, communicating over his headset, but they kept telling him to be quiet because they were getting an important weather report. When he finally got the message across, one of them came back, fixed the problem, and went back to the cockpit, saying "Just don't light a cigarette."

We flew out over the Ross Sea and up the coast of Victoria Land. The mountains were surrounded by white, seeming almost to be islands. In reality they act something like a dam holding back the ice. We came to a glacier called the Drygalski Ice Tongue and turned inland. Flying over this plain white river of ice gave me a moment of appreciation for the men who went to the Pole. In the presence of the white immensity, awe of their absurd courage was inescapable.

At the first site, weather station Sushila, we landed smoothly. The temperature was about minus 4 degrees. With all the cold-weather gear on I was toasty. The snow was powdery, the sun bright. The next site was Lynn. Here the temperature was about zero with the wind at 20 knots, nothing I hadn't experienced before in upstate New York, or Maine. But perhaps because of the isolation it seemed colder. For 360 degrees in all directions was a white plain with no hint of structure or variation, no comprehensible detail of any sort.

Or perhaps it was that we—well, Stearns and his assistant—were trying to work, to replace a weather vane, which required undoing nuts and bolts and using a screwdriver and pliers. Agile fingers were necessary, mittens were not useful, and with a wind chill of minus 40 it was simply too cold to keep naked fingers flexible.

At the third site I looked around and stared south. We were past the mountains and the glaciers, the polar plateau was ahead of us, the Pole about 700 miles away, a long day's drive on a freeway. In the direction of the Pole it was pure white. In the Twin Otter on the way back to McMurdo, lulled by the warmth and the rattle of machinery, which had come to seem like a kind of lullaby, I fell asleep.

* * *

The second trip was to the dry valleys, one of the most remarkable and unearthly places on earth, as remote from the ocean as one could get. At least on the polar plateau one was standing on water; one felt the nature of Antarctica to be water-bound in its frozen state, as unyielding to life as it was nurturing in the sea around the continent. In the dry valleys it was as if you had encountered the old bones of the earth, the dry heart of a world that had no interest in you, no awareness of you, no hope or pleasure to offer you, only the comfort of silence and indifference.

The dry valleys are located in the Transantarctic Mountains, 25 to 30 miles inland from the eastern edge of McMurdo Sound. They are free of snow and have only small tongues of glaciers licking at them. They also hold a number of strange freshwater lakes. Our destination was Lake Bonney. I flew in with Donal Manahan and John Welborn, his graduate student, on a navy helicopter. We flew in over the mountains, which are laced with glaciers.

As the helicopter set down on the shore at Lake Bonney the blow from the rotors sent glass ice that had formed on top of open water spinning in the air, flashing like silverfish and roiling the surface of the water. Lake Bonney, like most of the lakes in the dry valleys, is permanently ice-covered, but in summer there is a 20-foot moat around it where water has melted. The researchers camped at Lake Bonney in tents, with huts for kitchen, office, and laboratory space. They had an outhouse and crossed the moat in a small aluminum rowboat pulled by a rope at stem and stern. Rising on either side of the lake were rough peaks. All around the lake the land surface was exposed rather than covered with ice and snow. There were wide expanses of bare dirt, scattered with small and large boulders carved by the wind—ventifacts.

The Taylor Valley, in which Bonney lies, deeply quiet and lifeless, was stark and beautiful. It made the West of Ireland look like the rain forest. The apparent purity of the location, the sense of distance from humanity, was so strong as to be disorienting. On the other hand, the camp itself was as ugly as all the other evidences of human beings in Antarctica. It consisted of a Jamesway—the modern version of an Iroquois longhouse—barrels of chemicals, and a generator making a mechanical, combustive racket.

This juxtaposition of the ugly and the serene, the natural and the mechanical, silence and noise, is my enduring memory of the continent of Antarctica and the Southern Ocean. If you travel officially, and reasonably safely in the Antarctic, the sound of machinery is difficult to escape. There are remote camps, but few people get to them. For most of the visitors to the continent, particularly the military personnel and also the civilian support workers, the continent is a kind of illusion. Nature at its most powerful, most majestic, most holy if you are religiously inclined, is just out of reach, like a mirage. Without motor vehicles you can't safely escape the presence of McMurdo. With them, you can't get to the silence.

We were there to take samples of the water in Lake Bonney. The researchers camped there were studying microorganisms that lived in the lake. The lakes in the dry valleys are unusual in that they are static, and the water in them stays stratified. In Bonney, below 20 meters there is no oxygen, and the salinity is ten times that of seawater. Divers can't go down. Some of the other lakes have poisonous sulfur dioxide that can be absorbed through the skin. And some have laughing gas.

Even though my ostensible interest was in the ocean, there was no way I could pay attention to the gathering of samples and the discussions of the science. There was no way even to think about the ocean and the icebreaker lying offshore, waiting. I should have been out pursuing the ocean. But once in Antarctica, it does not pay to be too responsible about your original agenda. If you have a chance to go somewhere, you go. And once in one of the dry valleys it is impossible to think about anything other than the place you are in.

At midnight, Welborn and a friend of his who was working at Lake Bonney went off on a hike. The sun was perfectly bright; there was no night here anymore than there was at McMurdo. I wandered around a bit, looking at distant glaciers. There was no sense of scale here, and a snowbank that looked to be about 15 feet high and a couple of hundred yards away turned out to be a 100-foot-high glacier about 2 miles away.

The valleys are not truly dead. There are meltwater streams that cut through the bare dirt, with algae growing in them. In the lakes there is phytoplankton. There are even nematodes in the dirt. Indeed there have been enough human visitors to these remote valleys that the population of nematodes has changed. Human beings have brought in new nematodes with them. In some spots on Antarctica—like Cape Royds, where there is a huge penguin colony—nematodes from Scott's ponies have changed the microbiological ecology of the site. In the dry valleys anything that is left, organic or inorganic, is preserved. This is where mummified seals are found. We saw one in the ice of the lake, gradually melting its way through.

Sleeping was difficult, with the light streaming through the tent. Researchers in the field often succumb to what they call "the big eye." Because of the short time they have, the big workload, and the constant light, they often fall off a daily sleep-work schedule and work and sleep at unpredictable hours, cycling freely according to how they feel or how much work they have. They get the big eye.

Eventually I did fall asleep. In the morning military time returned briefly as we waited for the helicopter. When the helicopter landed, we had to be ready to jump on with all our gear. If this meant that because of delays you had to sit on your duff for three hours, that was life in the Antarctic. We ate, talked, had hot chocolate, discussed the recycling of human waste.

The dry valleys are a sensitive location, because nothing decays or leaves, so all human waste has to be taken out by helicopter, a job that has fallen to the navy pilots. Urine simply flowed down a funnel into a U-barrel that could be tightly capped and loaded on a helicopter. Solid waste was bagged. The traditional one-hole outhouse at Bonney was fitted out with a large plastic bag. The theory was that the people in remote camps would close the bag when it was somewhat full, but this ignored certain problems of social engineering, namely, who was going to bag and carry someone else's shit. At Bonney the custom was one bag per visit to the outhouse. This used up more plastic bags, but it reduced stress.

The helicopter landed and then took off again, to return in three hours. Welborn and I took a hike. We climbed over a landscape that seemed completely devoid of life. The colors of the crumbled rock were red, brown, gray. Distances were impossible to judge. A ridge that looked to be a quarter of a mile away was really a mile or more, with several hidden dips to cross to get to it.

The hills were scattered with ventifacts of all sizes. Some were mere polished pebbles. Others were giant Henry Moore sculptures, big enough to climb on and sit in. The holes that the wind had carved into stone often looked like eyes and mouths. One boulder brought to mind Munch's *Scream*, which seemed appropriate. When the wind howled down the valley in winter, doing its work, the openmouthed rock would be there, no one to see it, to think that it was screaming, silently. But this was all a kind of romantic image-making, really. In this place it was clear, perfectly so, that Plato was indeed wrong. The imagination was feeble compared to the reality, language brittle in the face of silence.

Chapter 6

HIGHER FORMS

Invertebrate larvae of the sort that inhabit the McMurdo aquarium along with other plankton—diatoms and algae—make up the base of the Southern Ocean ecosystem, a layer only accessible through the microscope, through the study of water samples, through the lens, literal and figurative, of science.

The Southern Ocean compared to a tropical rain forest, for instance, is rich but less complex. There are fewer species, but many individuals. It has several communities. One on the surface, dominated by krill and other crustaceans that are eaten by birds and seals and whales; and another on the bottom, of sponges and sea urchins, sea stars, and other invertebrates. Most of the fish live near the bottom and are relatively sedentary. Some are known only because they have been recovered from the stomachs of seals. And finally there are the communities of algae, microbes, plankton, and krill that live in the ice. Not on it, or around it, but in it.

The community of invertebrates on the bottom (below about 150 feet, where no bottom ice forms) is "one of the most species-rich, diverse and dense benthic communities on earth," according to Sanford Moss.[1] Almost nothing eats these bottom living creatures, so, as Spock on "Star Trek" would have said, they live long and prosper. One species of starfish, *Anasterias rupicola*, is known to reach an age of thirty-nine years.

Some other species, however, have the opposite adaptation. They are dwarfs, because of the difficulty of getting calcium out of the water. They also do not spend their reproductive capital lightly, producing few young and tending to brood them, to give them a better chance of survival. Many of these creatures are opportunists, eating anything organic. There is a wonderful word for this dietary catholicism: "planktivory."

The community of fish in the Antarctic regions of the Southern Ocean is less rich in species. Most of them live near the bottom. Most are endemic to the Antarctic—they are found nowhere else. And most are in one order, the Nototheniiformes. There are more than 11,000 species of saltwater fish. About 8,000 of these live in shallow, warm seas, about 3,400 in cold waters. Only 120 species live south of the Antarctic Convergence, with many more in the waters around the subantarctic islands like South Georgia.

Indeed, fishing rights off South Georgia have become a major political and environmental issue. Already, fishing off that island and Kerguelen had been active enough to deplete some of the stocks of marbled Antarctic rock cod and mackerel ice-fish during the 1970s and 1980s. Russia and Japan have sent fishing boats farther south to the Antarctic, although most of the fish they harvest are not intended for human consumption. Harvesting Antarctic fish is a cause for worry not because there is a clear danger to these fish, but because no one seems to know much about them. But, like many other organisms in the cold waters, Antarctic fish do have slow growth patterns and take a long time to reach maturity. They are also not fecund, laying few eggs, for fish that is—a few hundred to a few thousand. An Atlantic cod, by comparison, may produce up to 6 million eggs per year, and the cod fishery seems to be on the verge of collapse.[2]

The eggs of Antarctic fish are large, and the farther south the fish live, the larger the eggs are, the more yolk to give the young a head start. Many fish spawn in winter. The yolk carries the fish until the spring plankton bloom occurs. In the Antarctic, as in the Arctic, most of the growing and eating occur in spring and summer. But the Arctic is far richer in fish. Indeed, there are no oceangoing shoals of fish in the Antarctic. And fish consume only about 100 million tons of krill a year, far less than the birds or seals or whales.[3]

One of the more intriguing aspects of Antarctic fish is their natural antifreeze. Some fish can tolerate temperatures down to 20 degrees. Several scientists have studied these fish at McMurdo and discovered substances in their blood—glycoproteins—that stave off the formation of ice crystals.

The nineteenth-century explorers undertook enormous surveys of the ocean and accumulated many more specimens than anyone could effectively catalogue and study. Ross dredged to 400 fathoms and beyond. He described 234 species and predicted that life would be found at all depths.

The ice fishes, of the family Channichthyidae, form what is probably the most common and best known group. There are about fifteen species, and they are caught at 100 to 700 meters. They have no scales, feed on other fish, and grow up to 67 centimeters. These fish have no hemoglobin, so their blood is colorless and their gills are not red, but off-white. They have one-tenth to one-ninetieth the red blood cells of most fishes. Hemoglobin and red blood cells are important in bringing oxygen to the tissues, a fundamental process of life. But these fish survive with these apparent handicaps because, first, a cold-blooded creature in cold water has a low metabolism, and second, the water in the Southern Ocean has ample supplies of oxygen. (Even other Antarctic fish that do have hemoglobin have small amounts and fewer red blood cells than fishes that live in warmer oceans.) Ice fish also have a greater volume of blood, a larger heart, and larger gills than other fish, as well as a skin that is adapted to allow absorption of oxygen directly from the water.

The fishes of the Antarctic memorialize explorers in their Latin names. There is *Prionadraco evansi,* after Edgar Evans, who died with Scott on the way back from the Pole. This is one of the dragon fishes and is semitransparent. You can see blood vessels, gills, and vertebrae through the skin. There is *Pagothenia borchgrevinki,* which feeds on the underside of sea ice, named after Carsten Borchgrevink, the Norwegian explorer who traveled to the Antarctic on two expeditions and was the first to make a sled journey on the Ross Ice Shelf. And *Pogronphryne scotti,* the plunder fish, named after Scott himself. Some other fish, with common names as rich as the Latin, are eel pouts, rat tails, sea snails, and eel cods.

Charles Wilkes, the American naval officer who led the ill-fated United States Exploring Expedition (he sailed in 1838 with six ships and returned in 1842 with two), collected fish in the Antarctic, off the South Shetlands and South America, Australia, and New Zealand. He gave the collection to the great American biologist Louis Agassiz at Harvard. But Agassiz could not complete an analysis of the specimens. As often occurs with field collections, the money for the expedition was there, but the money for study after the fact was harder to come by.

The biological hero of the Southern Ocean is krill. Krill is a small, shrimplike creature that is one of the many crustaceans, such as copepods and amphipods, that feed on plankton and in turn become food for birds, seals, and whales. To read ecological studies of the ecosystem of the Southern Ocean is to read ode upon ode to krill.

There are only two main species in the Southern Ocean.

Most krill species are actually found in tropical and subtropical waters. But, in characteristic Antarctic fashion, while the number of species is small, the number of individuals is enormous. Estimates of annual krill production vary wildly—from 135 million tons to 1.35 billion tons—but are all great.[4]

Still, krill are a substantial mystery, and the variations in the numbers indicate the lack of knowledge. It was suggested in the 1970s, for instance, that an annual catch of 150 million tons would be possible. That is roughly 50 million tons more than all the creatures that are now taken each year from every sea and ocean in the world.[5]

Some stretches of water are barren of krill. And in other places they may occur in swarms with concentrations as high as 60,000 individuals, or 35 kilograms, per cubic meter of water. These swarms may have several functions, enabling reproduction, or feeding, or the transmission of signals about predators. What could a swarm of krill do if, say, a blue whale were about to swim through, vacuuming them up. Some divers have reported seeing a school of krill molt all at once, shedding their exoskeletons in an instant. This may be a ruse to distract predators.[6]

Of all krill, *Euphausia superba*, the superb euphausid, is the most widespread and best studied. It was first fully described by James D. Dana, one of the officers who accompanied Charles Wilkes on the United States Exploring Expedition. He published his work in 1855. This one species accounts for about half of the zooplankton in the surface layer.

Krill spawn from January to March. Their eggs sink and hatch at a depth of about 750 meters, in water warmer than the surface. As the larvae develop they move closer to the surface. They reach 6 centimeters over two or three years, a life span that makes them planktonic Methuselahs. They swim by paddling their tails, and *Superba* is a fast swimmer, with a high metabolism and an omnivorous appetite. It eats whatever it can get, from microorganisms to other crustaceans.

On the next rung of the surface layer food chain are the birds. They eat krill, of course, and copepods and other crustaceans; and the albatrosses and the king penguins eat squid; and the giant petrels eat anything. The spectacular flowering of bird life is one of the great thrills of the Southern Ocean, the primary signal to a traveler that the ocean is not cold and barren, but cold and fecund. Indeed, Rachel Carson pointed out in 1950 in *The Sea Around Us* that in the tropics there are no dense swarms of surface plankton, and as a consequence tropical seas do not have the "clouds of shearwaters, fulmars, auks, whalebirds, albatrosses, and other birds" that bring cold seas to life.[7]

One tends to find these clouds of birds, as any fisherman knows, where the food is, whether it is krill, or copepods, or squid. Near islands or the ice edge there are always clouds of birds. Indeed birds are often a sign of land, or of ice. In *The Wreck of the Favorite*, a sailor of the nineteenth century wrote that he and his mates were delighted to see albatrosses and petrels. "We regarded them as one travelling over a dreary desert would view the inhabitants of some city widely separated from the rest of the world, and to which he might be approaching."[8]

Sailors and travelers, naturalists and explorers, have given different birds different personalities, most notably in the case of the albatross. The late Robert Cushman Murphy, curator of ornithology at the American Museum of Natural History, was one of those extraordinary men who have a gift for language as well as science. His description of his first sighting of a great albatross deserves quoting in full:

> Much that is well heralded in nature carries a tinge of disappointment when it is finally found. A few things, on the other hand, seem beyond over-advertisement. When I faced my first big tree in California, expectation sank into nothingness. The feeling was similar when for the first time I watched and heard the dual performance of the Skylark. With a handful of such

> experiences, in which reality can hardly fail to transcend hope, I would group the sighting of a great albatross at sea.
>
> For me the event came in latitude 23 S, longitude 35 45 W, off Rio de Janeiro, on October 28, 1912. We had just encountered an abrupt change from tropical weather, and a heavy ground swell indicated storms to southward. At six o'clock in the morning the steward of the 'Daisy' came to notify me that a 'Gony' was about, so I hurried on deck. Near-by, in the morning sunlight, flew the long anticipated fowl, even more majestic, more supreme in its element than my imagination had pictured. It was mature, all white and black, doubtless an adult male, and as it turned and turned, now flashing the bright under side, now showing the black that extended from wrist to tip on the upper surface of the wings, the narrow planes seemed to be neither beating nor scarcely quivering. Lying on the invisible currents of the breeze, the bird appeared merely to follow its pinkish bill at random.[9]

Watching albatrosses in flight is a meditative exercise. Even the smaller albatrosses, often called mollymauks (there are about fourteen species altogether), drift and glide in perfect display. The only hint that the albatross is exerting control over its flight is the movement of its feet, which are used like ailerons or rudders.

Most of us have in our minds, when we hear the name of the bird, the albatross from Coleridge's poem (an albatross that was shot with a crossbow in the Southern Ocean), in particular the image of the bird hung around the mariner's neck. Sailors made him wear it around his neck because he had killed "the bird / That made the breeze to blow."

A telling perception, but perhaps the wrong way round. The evolutionary point of view would be that it was the breeze that made the bird to glide. Whether one is poetic, superstitious, or scientific, it is clear that albatrosses live by and with the wind. The wandering albatross circumnavigates the globe on steady westerlies, riding air currents, climbing, soaring, diving, tracing the contours of long swells. In its youth, a great albatross rests on the surface of the sea and does not touch land for years. Albatrosses have been tracked flying 3,000 miles in ten days.

At the opposite end of the metaphorical order is Wilson's storm petrel, which Murphy called "Mother Carey's Chicken." Unlike the lordly albatross, the storm petrel is small. It has a wingspan of about 16 inches, as opposed to 11 feet. It does not glide; it flies like a peasant with a sore back. It beats the air. It steps on the water to help itself along. You can see its feet tap, tap, tap on the crests of swells, giving itself a boost to fly over them. And yet with all its apparent labor in flight, it manages to breed each year in Antarctica and travels as far north as New England's latitudes during the northern summer. In seafaring legend the souls of drowned sailors are reincarnated as albatrosses, while drowned landlubbers are doomed to come back as storm petrels.

I saw both albatrosses and storm petrels at sea. And I saw them on their nests on land, the albatrosses on South Georgia and the storm petrels on Signy Island in the South Orkneys. These latter are near the northern tip of the archipelago of islands that extends out from the Antarctic peninsula, indicating the underwater mountain range, bent by continental drift, that extends from the Andes to Antarctica. Signy is a rough chunk of rock with numerous fur seals and moss banks 4,000 years old.

It is as rough and craggy a place as one can imagine. The petrel, so seemingly fragile, so apparently at the mercy of such fierce elements, had made its nest in a cleft in a rock wall. Just briefly, I looked into the crevice and saw the dark, barely visible eye of the bird and glimpsed an egg. I felt a small shock. For a moment the stories of storm petrels slipped from my mind, along with their migratory routes and reproductive habits, and Latin and English names. It was as if somehow I had just bumped up against the world itself, instead of my version of it.

I seemed to be looking through clear, instead of clouded, glass, aware only of the white egg, dusky brown-gray feathers, and limpid brown eye. For a moment I was outside of myself, in the present, simply there with the storm petrel.

I have a preference, perhaps willfully contrary, for the hard-working little bird over the great soaring one. I'm a landsman, after all, not a sailor. I know where my soul is going to end up if I'm lost at sea. And my life, and that of everyone else I know, is far more like that of the petrel than that of the albatross. We struggle to fly, staying just above the surface, tapping the swells with our feet.

There are other birds whose characters, as humans see them, inform and enliven the Southern Ocean: the giant petrel, for instance, otherwise known as the great-winged petrel, or more familiarly, Uncle Nasty. I heard that term from a penguin specialist looking down from a cliff on one of the South Orkney Islands at a giant petrel that had just pulled its red bloodied head from the carcass of a dead seal. Uncle Nasty is a scavenger, the size of a smaller albatross, but with a less elegant pattern of flight. It is brown and undistinguished looking, with a chunkier body.

Another bird that cannot be ignored is the skua, a large gull-like creature that haunts penguin colonies. It does not have the talons or beak of a dedicated predator, but it is clever and strong. It steals penguin eggs and kills penguin chicks that have wandered off by themselves. Sometimes a pair of skuas will work in tandem to get a penguin off an egg or away from a chick.

There is the sheath bill, a waddling, chickenlike bird with unpleasant habits. It is an omnivore. It eats regurgitated fish that the penguin chicks miss, seal feces, placentas and after-birth of seals, and any other organic material it can find. It is found very far south and haunts human habitations, as do the skuas.

And then there is the penguin, the bird that most characterizes the Southern Ocean. Just consider one astonishing statistic. When you estimate the biomass (or weight) of all the birds south of the Antarctic Convergence the figure is about 200 million tons. That's more than sixty species from petrels, to gulls, to the disgusting sheath bill. Of all that bird flesh, all but 3 million tons are penguins. And two-thirds of those penguins are Adelies, the little men in white tie and tails. Above the convergence, in the subantarctic, penguins are still 80 percent of the bird biomass. Half of those penguins are macaronis. Their populations are very evident during the summer at any Antarctic island. But during the winter they go to sea, where they are seldom seen.

There are seventeen or eighteen species of penguins, depending on how you count them, and it is a fitting testimony to the elusiveness of the ocean itself that a bird whose life is in the water, whose body is designed for the water, is known primarily for its awkwardness on land. If penguins did not look like toddlers, they would be no more popular than elephant seals. They smell almost as bad and make a good deal more noise. It is in the water, porpoising, swimming with force and elegance, flying underwater with their flippers, that penguins are most themselves. Or so I am willing to claim, since the penguins cannot write their own books.

If there is one thing that penguins signal about the Southern Ocean, it is abundance. On the Antarctic peninsula tens of thousands of the birds will gather in one place to nest and mate. These colonies can be seen from a mile or more offshore. If they are hidden from view, you can smell them before you arrive, because the penguins stand and walk and nest in their own excrement, all the while squawking madly and enforcing territorial boundaries. In the harshest terrain, including the continental ice shelf itself, one finds penguin colonies, noisy cities insisting on the ocean's abundance.

It was thought once that penguins were primitive birds; indeed, *The Worst Journey in the World,* by Apsley Cherry-Garrard, is an account of a trip, made during Scott's second and last Antarctic expedition, to collect an egg of an emperor penguin, which it was believed would shed light on the evolution of birds. Emperors nest in the dark of winter on the ice shelves of Antarctica. So retrieving the egg required either heroism or foolhardiness, depending on one's point of view.

Though the expedition's stated purpose was scientific, the trip was also a warmup early in the expedition for the later trek to the Pole. And something more than the need for data impelled the three men—Garrard, William Wilson, and "Birdie" Bowers—to drag loaded sleds in temperatures as cold as minus 70 degrees. In no way, even by the science of the time and the understanding of the participants, was the egg worth the hardship and risk of life that they underwent. Sometimes the three men made only a mile in a day. Their parkas froze around them as soon as they emerged from the tent (which had a stove in it). Their sleeping bags were frozen at night when they crawled into them. At one point they lost their tent in a storm.

All survived this trip, but Wilson and Bowers later perished with Scott on the way back from the South Pole. Garrard dutifully brought the egg to the British Museum of Natural History. He had trouble even getting anyone to take it, and reports in the postscript to his book that it never was really studied.

Neither Garrard nor any of his contemporaries knew that penguins are not at all primitive. Penguins evolved fairly recently, about 50 million years ago, apparently from birds like today's diving petrels that could both fly and swim. Gradually they adapted to the seas; their swimming improved, and their wings became ill-suited to the air, adapted to the thicker medium of water. Penguins also developed heavier bones and a hydrodynamically efficient shape.

Nor are penguins Antarctic birds above all, although that is their reputation. They range as far north as the Equator and first evolved for life in cold temperate seas. Only later did species like the emperor and Adelie become particularly adapted to the deep cold of the Antarctic.

Far south, penguins and seals are the only forms of life to break the tyranny of geology and glaciology. As you move farther north, to the islands above or near the Antarctic Convergence, the penguins are still there in prodigious numbers, but then all bird and animal life explodes in noisy profusion. Apart from whaling, which is no longer possible, there is probably no way to feel quite as vividly the richness of the ocean other than to visit one of these islands. For me, South Georgia, 1,000 miles east and north of the Antarctic peninsula, was the most spectacular spot in my travels in the Southern Ocean. In fact it is the most beautiful, most moving place I have ever seen.

Of course, the beholder's eye always influences his reaction. I arrived at South Georgia after two weeks on my first trip to the Antarctic. I was recovering from something halfway between bronchitis and pneumonia, and had found the Antarctic peninsula's grimness extremely unwelcoming. And just as I was returning to the living, the ship arrived off South Georgia, with birds everywhere—prions, petrels, gulls, penguins—and seals leaping dolphinlike 50 yards from the ship.

The first stop was at Cooper Island, one of many small, rocky outcrops around South Georgia itself. The air was warm, in the 40s, and as we went ashore in an inflatable boat with outboard motor, black-browed albatrosses flew in the hundreds in the air and rafted together in flocks on the water. Macaroni penguins frolicked on the surface, lying on their backs and preening their feathers. A seal swam by the boat. We could see the green tussock grass, and the chatter of the penguins sounded like the bleating of goats.

More surprising, there were some sort of small, flying insects. Never have insects inspired such elation in me. I felt as if I were returning to the planet Earth. After a first landing where the rocks were simply too slippery and steep for human beings—the penguins did fine—I went with a small group to another beach. Here there were beds of kelp and a meltwater stream that we followed up to a grassy hill. Ducks—South Georgia pintails—were in the air, and the green cliff was sprinkled with nesting albatrosses.

At the top of the cliff we looked out on the wind-tossed bay, with hundreds of albatrosses in the sky along with ducks and the little South Georgia pipit, the island's only land bird. One nesting albatross, not 10 feet away, sat serene, with delicate brows, as if drawn by eyeliner. The chicks were all soft gray, still in their down, with a black line around the eye and black, black beaks.

This first landing left me stunned with the impact of so much life, so visible, so close, so beautiful. It was like falling in love, or coming home. There was none of the subtle pleasure of coming to a moment of pure consciousness in the presence of the natural world. The feeling was more like a shout of joy, not a loss of self, but a reawakening of self, a biological rather than a philosophical satisfaction.

And this exhilaration of returning home, this biophilic surge, was followed by one experience after another of the same sort. We landed among a colony of king penguins, the most beautiful penguins, and among the most beautiful of all birds, tall and slender, with black feet and silver backs, black hoods and orange and yellow splashes. To and from the penguin colony, fur seals, like large dogs, chased us with teeth bared, running on their elbows. To fend them off we kicked sand at them or threw pebbles. Elephant seals, enormous and smelly, lay molting on the beach.

The penguins were gathered 50,000 strong on Salisbury Plain. In the rain they stood hunched over the eggs that they kept on their feet, evenly spaced, as if they were on stationary nests. Later, on a trip by Bird Island, a small island lying off the main island, we listened to hordes of adolescent seals hooting and barking like drunk teenagers on a summer night. They climbed cliffs 100 feet high. At another spot we hiked in among the nests of wandering albatrosses. I sat next to one of these birds, with a wingspan of 11 feet or so, a bill 8 inches long, and gradually moved closer to it on its nest until I reached out and touched it with the tip of my finger, as gently as possible. It reached down, like a pet parakeet, and nibbled gently on the finger, although it probably could have taken it off.

When upset, albatrosses vomit a vile liquid at the creature bothering them, usually an ornithologist. The birds know no land predators, and no predators in the air, and just about no predators in the sea. They are consequently serene, perhaps in a permanent meditative state, or perhaps they are simply not that bright.

On a day when the temperature reached into the 60s, we landed at Gritvyken Harbor and hiked along the beach and up a cliff covered with tussock grass to look down at a sea the color of the Caribbean and watch light-mantled sooty albatrosses courting on the wing, flying in unison, dipping and turning, the male trying to get the female to land at the nest he had picked out on the cliffs. When they left their nests they did not launch themselves, they just spread their wings and fell off into the air.

We also visited Strom Ness Harbor, where we dined in the abandoned whalers' mess. On a walk into the foothills, our guide dug a white-chinned petrel out of a muddy burrow set in a hill covered with all sorts of mosses. On the ridges we saw reindeer, brought to the island by Norwegian whalers. On the main island there were no pipits. They had been wiped out by rats, also brought by whalers.

Strom Ness is famous for something other than whaling and bird life; it was the end point of Ernest Shackleton's famous open boat voyage from Elephant Island, where a small party left the rest of their crew after their ship, the *Endeavor,* was crushed in the ice. Shackleton, Frank Worsley as navigator, and four other men sailed 800 miles in a 20-foot open boat, the *James Caird.* They survived freezing temperatures and storms with huge seas. The men would crawl up on the bow to chop the salty ice. Their wet and dirty sleeping bags began to ferment—a benefit, because it produced heat. When they finally reached South Georgia they encountered hurricane conditions, not uncommon around the island. We had spectacular sunny days, but on an earlier visit, the same cruise ship had anchored off South Georgia in force twelve conditions. Winds of 100 miles per hour kept the tourists in their cabins. Nobody could even emerge to get to the dining room. Stewards on the ship had to crawl on their hands and knees down the corridors to bring cold food to the passengers.

When Shackleton and his group finally landed, they were on the wrong side of the island. The whaling settlements were on the other side. Shackleton, Worsley, and Tom Crean proceeded to climb over mountains and glaciers to the settlements, leaving the rest of their party to set up a camp and wait. The climbing party put screws through the soles of their boots in lieu of crampons, gathered rope, and made the attempt. Eventually they came to a point on a glacier where they could not turn back, and ahead of them was a slope of ice that plunged down in darkness. They coiled their rope into a makeshift sled and the three of them sat on it, holding one another around the waist, and pushed off into the darkness. They survived, unscathed. In later days they always said they felt a fourth man had been with them.

They then trudged on to the whaling camp at Strom Ness. In a book on whaling written in the 1950s, a British physician recounted the comments of an old whaleman who claimed to have been at Strom Ness when Shackleton came down from the mountains. By Worsley's account and Shackleton's own, the three men were black with dirt, their clothes ragged, beards long, and faces gaunt; they were unrecognizable even though they had been to this whaling camp and were known to the manager. The whaleman described it this way: "Manager say: 'Who the hell are you?' and terrible bearded man in the center of the three say very quietly: 'My name is Shackleton.' Me—I turn away and weep. I think manager weep, too."[10]

The manager's house is still there, a ramshackle affair of weatherbeaten wood. The site is filled with rusting tanks and machinery and tumbledown buildings. In a way this one place embodies the human interaction with the Southern Ocean. Standing on the beach looking inland you can see the detritus of whaling, and farther, beyond the moss-covered hills, the saddle in the mountains where Shackleton's glacier is visible. Or you can turn seaward to watch the penguins waddle, the seals wallow in the surf, and the terns dip and tilt in the air under high-stacked clouds formed by the offshore winds.

Chapter 7

WHALING

If any antidote is still needed to the notion that technological innovation equals progress, the story of whaling in the Antarctic ought to provide it. The sealers killed their prey without restraint or forethought and all but managed to destroy them, even though they worked with clubs and lances and the sparing rifle shot. The early whalers hunted the sperm and right whales in boats powered and harpoons launched by men's arms and shoulders. They caused considerable havoc, but they were hunters with limited power. In the first collision between the Southern Ocean and the hungry machinery of commerce, the fecundity and vastness of the ocean was set against primitive technique. The seals found places to hide. They reproduced. The ocean fed them as it always had.

In the twentieth century, with the advent of the harpoon gun and the motorized whale catcher, the balance of power swung widely out of control. The wholesale mechanized killing and processing of whales began with as little sense or regulation as it had in the killing of the seals, but the whales reproduced more slowly and had fewer places to hide. The sealers, like Sherman in Georgia, practiced total war. But Sherman rode on horseback. The twentieth-century Antarctic whalers had the bomb.

It is also arguable that the sealers really didn't know the extent of the damage they were causing. The ocean must have seemed nearly infinite to them. And certainly the New England investors who funded the seal hunt and the landsmen who rode ships south to execute it had no scientists to chart population decline and issue reports and recommendations.

The whalers did. Even when it was clear that the whales were disappearing, the whaling companies did not hold back.

The story of Southern Ocean whaling in the twentieth century is one of technical sophistication and willful ecological ignorance. Whaling companies brought the Industrial Revolution to the killing seas. For many of the men involved, those who did not ride the chase boats and shoot the harpoon guns but who worked in the factories on land or onboard the big mother ships, the whaling business was simply Chaplin's *Modern Times*, in which the factory where the tramp works threatens to overwhelm him. Except that in a whaling factory the workers stood knee-deep in blubber and blood. If Chaplin had done *Modern Times* on a whaling ship no one would have laughed. Perhaps the proper chronicler of factory whaling would have been Sinclair Lewis. He could have written the modern successor to *Moby Dick*, recounting in excruciating detail the processing of blubber, meat, and bone.

Whaling in the Southern Ocean did not begin in the twentieth century, of course. It began with sperm whales, which were named for spermaceti, a liquid wax that came from the head and was used to make smokeless candles. Like the right whale before it, the sperm whale was also hunted for its blubber, which was boiled down to make oil. Sperm whales produce the finest oil of any whale. It was prized for lamps and lubrication.

The whalers' destinations were more often the warm southern Pacific seas than the colder latitudes. English whalers were the first to round the Horn in 1789, and the Americans followed two years later. These ships were hunting sperm and right whales, both slow enough to be pursued by men rowing small boats. Other whales, the rorquals, or baleen whales—fin, sei, and blue—were too fast to pursue.

There was some sperm whaling off the coasts of Peru and Chile, and by 1802 off New Zealand and in the Indian Ocean, off islands like Kerguelen. Often, one ship hunted whales, fur seals, and elephant seals. Joseph Fuller, shipwrecked on Kerguelen, was on such a ship. The so-called Golden Age of Yankee sperm whaling began after the War of 1812. The whalers hunted in the Indian Ocean, off Japan, off Madagascar and Seychelles. In 1842 more than 594 U.S. ships were whaling.[1] In 1846 there were 729 American whaling vessels on the high seas and 70,000 men employed in whaling.

But sperm whales had become harder to find. Then industry began to produce oil from minerals, and the miracle of petroleum-based oils removed the main economic base for the hunt. By the American Civil War, sperm whaling was a minor industry. The small amount of sperm oil produced was used to lubricate watches and fine machine parts. The hunt continued as an anachronism, something like beaver trapping, until about 1912.

The invention of the harpoon gun by a Norwegian whaler named Svend Foyn in 1868 made modern whaling possible. Added to the power of this innovation was the speed of whale catchers powered first by steam and then by diesel engines. These whale catchers could successfully pursue the huge and fast rorquals, most of all the blue and fin whales. The catchers fed their kill to shore whaling factories on South Georgia at Strom Ness and Grytviken. Whale catchers went to sea, killed whales, and brought them back to the island to be processed.

The rorquals did not float when dead the way sperm and right whales did. They had to be inflated with a hose and air compressor, like a beach ball, and then towed in.

A Norwegian invented the harpoon gun, and a Norwegian started using it in Antarctic waters. C. A. Larsen first tried whaling in the Weddell Sea in 1892–93 with no great success. Then he brought the Swedish South Polar Expedition to Antarctica in 1901. After setting explorers off on Antarctic soil he took his ship, the *Antarctica*, to the Falklands and South Georgia. The *Antarctica* was eventually crushed by ice, but Larsen, with Argentine backing, went home, outfitted two sailing ships and a steamship, and came back to Grytviken on South Georgia at the end of 1904 and set up the first whaling station.[2]

In 1905 the first factory ships, which processed whales at sea, began working off the South Shetland Islands along the Antarctic peninsula. These early ships, really revamped merchantmen, processed the whales over the side. Men climbed over the side of the ship and walked the whale with spiked boots, cutting off the blubber with long flensing knives. Deception Island was a popular spot for them to anchor out of the weather, since the island is a volcanic caldera protected on all sides, with one small entrance. Once stripped, the whale carcasses were cut adrift and washed up on shore, where they rotted.

Today Deception Harbor is a must-see for tourists. On my tour of the Antarctic peninsula we landed on Deception Island in rubber boats and walked among the enormous whale vertebrae and ribs, now white and dry, bleached by time into an austere reminder of the huge bodies that once lay rotting, to the delight of skuas and giant petrels. The volcano is not completely quiet, by the way. The water is still heated by its activity, and a favorite treat for tourists onboard nature cruises is to swim in the warm waters of Deception Harbor, then sip from thermoses of mixed drinks on the beach.

Hunting rorquals was a wholly different operation from sperm whaling, on shore or on factory ships. At South Georgia, on shore, butchering occurred on what was called the "plan," two acres that sloped toward the sea. This was where the process began that turned the great whales into margarine for Britain and Europe, and soap, textile and leather-tanning chemicals, oilcloth, and linoleum in the United States. As whaling progressed, and all of the whale came to be used, the meat and bones were also processed, sometimes as poultry food.

Robert Cushman Murphy, the great authority on seabirds of the Southern Hemisphere, visited South Georgia when factory whaling was in full swing. Murphy was not there to observe the whaling factories. He was a passenger on the last voyage of what was probably the last square-rigged sperm whaling ship out of New England, the *Daisy*, in 1911–12. He had only been married a few months, and he kept a journal for his new bride that he later published. It is called *Logbook for Grace*, and it is a wonderful piece of observation and writing: graceful, delicate, and forceful.

He describes coming into the island:

> The whole shoreline of Cumberland Bay proved to be lined for miles with the bones of whales, mostly humpbacks. Spinal columns, loose vertebrae, ribs, and jaws were piled in heaps and bulwarks along the waterline and it was easy to count a hundred huge skulls within a stone's throw.
>
> . . . The odor of very stale whale then increased again as we entered the cove, which might be likened to a great cauldron so filled with the rotting flesh and macerated bones of whales that they not only bestrew its bottom but also thickly encrust its rim to the farthest highwater mark.[3]

F. D. Ommaney, a member of the British Discovery Committee to investigate whaling, inspected the factory at Grytviken in the 1920s. He wrote: "This was the great charnel yard where the whales were stripped and dismembered and their fragments fed into the boilers." The board floor was covered in grease and slime. Steam winches and steam saws were used.

> When the plan was working to capacity it was a gory scene. Flesh and guts lay about like small hillocks and blood flowed in rivers amid the racket of the winches and the thrashing of the rotary knife that sliced the blubber. Steel wires whipped and tautened in all directions while clouds of steam from winches and boilers arose as from a giant cauldron.[4]

Work began at 5:30 A.M. The catchers would bring the whales in overnight and leave them—sometimes one or two whales, but sometimes twenty,

> . . . their grooved underparts upwards, swollen with the compressed air pumped into them, and now still more inflated by the gases of their own decomposition. The heads and tails were invisible beneath the greasy water so that they looked like enormous pumpkins. Multitudes of sea birds surrounded them, tearing at the blubber, fighting and screaming. At midsummer they speckled the surface of the harbour like leaves and their chatter and screaming, audible from afar, continued without ceasing day and night. This vast population of scavenging sea birds was entirely sustained by refuse from the whaling stations. Now that whaling in South Georgia has come to an end countless thousands of sea birds must have perished.[5]

While at the harbor of Grytviken, Murphy dined with Captain C. A. Larsen, "the King of Modern Whaling and the first to establish the industry or, as I prefer to say, 'exploitation,' in the oceans of the far South."[6] Larsen spared himself no comfort. Murphy dined with him one night on a luxurious eight-course meal, with beer and cigars, served by a butler. The whale men who worked in the factory made do with lesser fare, particularly for alcoholic beverages. One whale catcher had to come back to harbor because someone had drunk all the alcohol in its compass. The whale men drank brilliantine. And two methods of getting drunk on boot polish are reported. In one, you make a sandwich, spreading the polish on bread. In another, more delicate, the polish is heated to get the alcohol out.

In 1950, when whaling was well past its peak, but 12,000 men, almost all Norwegians, went to the Southern Ocean each year to hunt whales, a British psychiatrist, who had signed on a whaling expedition as a ship's doctor, visited South Georgia. He writes:

> I have been in Indian and African villages where sanitation is an unknown word, and where the villages raise themselves some inches higher every year on their own excreta; Leith Harbour is filthier than these. I have been in the slums of Glasgow, Cairo, Calcutta, and Shanghai; the denizens of those terrifying slums are better cared for by their fellow citizens than are the whalemen living in Leith Harbour cared for by anyone. I have seen soulless industrialization, evil money-grubbing by state or private company at the expense of human souls, in many parts of the world, but nothing so shameful have I seen as the total disregard by the whaling companies and the authorities of my own nation for anything but the production of more whale oil at Leith Harbour, no matter to what degrading depths man may be brought in the process.[7]

The island was known to whalers as the "slum of the Southern Ocean."

From the middle 1920s on, factory ships were equipped with slipways to haul carcasses on deck. In the 1930s factory ships of 20,000 to 25,000 tons were specially built for the job. Some even had amenities for the crew, such as showers.[8]

In some ways, factory ship whaling was reminiscent of earlier times. There was the search, in later years with helicopters; the pursuit of the whale; and the kill. But the equipment was far different, and the scale of the operation was so much bigger. When R. B. Robertson went south in the 1950s he accompanied an expedition of seventeen ships and 650 men. The strategy and tactics he describes were almost military in nature. One whale catcher led the hunt, searching the pack ice for whales. When the lead ship found whales, thirteen whale catchers would spread out over 50 miles in a curved net of sorts. The catchers killed whales, and other boats came up behind to attach buoys to the carcasses. Two other ships followed them to tow the carcasses to the factory ship. All parts of the operation kept in contact with one another by radio telephone. This was big business. An average whaling expedition was capitalized at about $8 million and returned a gross profit of $6 million or more.[9]

Harpooners on modern whale catchers were really gunners, and the gun they operated fired a harpoon with an explosive grenade at the tip. The gunner aimed for the backbone of the whale, between the shoulder blades. If the grenade missed shattering the backbone it would explode internally, and the sound of the explosion could be heard by those on deck.

Ommaney wrote:

> Several tough gunners told me they did not really like their job and had had about enough of it by the time the season came to an end. For a watcher such as myself, not yet inured to this spectacle of anguish, there is the difficulty of imagining that this grotesque creature, plunging and wallowing at the end of the line, is a beast as sentient as a horse and, in its own way, as noble. Its habit of life in its unfamiliar element makes it impersonal and mysterious. What an outcry there would have been long ago, as Sir Alister Hardy has remarked, if herds of great land mammals, say elephant or buffalo, were chased in armored vehicles firing explosive grenades from cannon, and then hauled close at the end of a line and bombarded again until dead![10]

His observations were echoed by Robertson, sailing in the 1950s, who was told by the captain of his whaling ship that all whaling gunners had ulcers. Robertson accompanied a whale catcher on the hunt and describes the scene. It was the messboy who spotted the whale, shouting *"Hvalblast! Hvalblast!"*

The catcher proceeded to chase the whales—blue whales. This catcher was equipped with a harpoon gun on swivel with a pistol grip, firing a 6-foot-long harpoon weighing 200 pounds. The grenade was set to explode three seconds after the harpoon was fired.

Robertson describes a scene of shouting and swearing, maneuvering, the canon shot sound of the harpoon gun, and "the dull detonation of the grenade inside the whale."[11] The line attached to the harpoon was run through a mast on the ship, so that the whale could be played like a fish if it did not die from the blast of the grenade. Twenty fathoms of 3-inch nylon rope ran from the harpoon to a stronger hemp rope. The mast took the strain, and a winch served the function of the reel. This whale dived. Each time it came to the surface the harpooner shot it again with another explosive harpoon. These harpoons had no line attached. Each shot brought spurts of blood from the whale.

When the great creature was finally dead, it was reeled in. The men on the catcher punctured its belly with a blubber spade at the end of a bamboo pole, inserted a pipe, and filled the belly with air. They also cut off the flukes, to prevent it twisting on the way in as it was towed. Sometimes the whales did not die alone. Even with motorized catchers and harpoon guns the whales could wreak revenge. Robertson describes one case in which a whale came up from a dive and threw a loose harpoon back toward the boat. That set off the gun so that it fired the harpoon that was at the ready into the harpooner, who lived only long enough to get back to the factory ship.

The scene at the shipboard charnel platform was much like that on the plan at South Georgia, but perhaps more efficient. The whales were pulled up the stern deck with a huge grab, or whale claw (*hval kla*). No longer were the whales flensed over the side as they had been in the early days of factory ships. And once onboard the entire carcass was consumed, a use found for every part. As soon as the whale was on the ship the flensers jumped on, made cuts, inserted toggles, and hauled out chunks of blubber. Then the "blubber boys" cut the whale up and sent the pieces down holes in the deck for boiling down. There were different holes for different parts of the whale. The meat went down one hole, the bones down another, the liver down yet another.

The Southern Ocean supports about twenty different species of whales and dolphins, including killer whales, or orcas, which were never hunted for profit, and sperm whales, the one large-toothed whale, which feed on giant squid. Antarctic whaling concentrated on the baleen whales—blue, pygmy blue, fin, sei, minke, humpback, and the southern right whale, which is rarely seen far south.

Whalers hunted all these creatures, but none so devotedly as the blue whale, the largest animal on earth and the most prized catch. Adult blue whales average 23 meters long and 100 tons. They can reach 30.5 meters and 200 tons. At that size the whale would reach near the length of Cook's ship, the *Resolution*, which measured 110 feet. Indeed, when whale catchers needed to tie up to the factory ship, they used whales as giant fenders to keep the ships from slamming into each other. Without a whale the whale catcher could not approach the mother ship. Blue whale calves are born live, weigh up to 3 tons at birth, and grow close to 4 centimeters and 80 kilograms a day while they are nursing. Each day, in other words, a blue whale calf gains the weight of a lineman in the National Football League. In three weeks it puts on the poundage of the entire Dallas Cowboys starting lineup.

The decline in the population of blue whales demonstrates, as does nothing else, the intensity and effectiveness of modern whaling. In the early years of the century there were probably 180,000 blue whales in the Southern Ocean. The hunt continued with one exception until 1963, when the International Whaling Commission introduced a ban on killing blue and humpback whales. The one break was provided by World War II, when human beings concentrated on killing one another. There was no whaling from 1940 to 1944. Now there are about 8,000 blue whales left.

The next biggest rorqual is the fin whale, which can weigh up to 90 tons and be 26 meters long. Since Antarctic whaling began, their population has declined from about 400,000 to 82,000. Then come the sei whales at about 20 meters long. These were considered small prey, and they were a disappointing catch.[12]

Problems with the whale harvest began early. First, the humpbacks started disappearing from catches and the sei whales increasing. That was in the 1920s. By 1930–31 the South Georgian annual catch was down to 8,000, but the overall Antarctic catch was 40,000. By this time it was quite clear that whaling was eating up its own livelihood. There were, for instance, many immature whales in the catch. Lack of adults is a sure sign of a population in trouble. Nothing changed. In 1937–38 whalers took 46,000. By 1953–54 the take was down to 31,000. And from 1957 to 1962 the average number of whales killed in a season was 33,000. Blue whales were then beginning to disappear.

By 1963 there was no whaling in South Georgia. The harbors were leased to the Japanese but soon shut down again in 1965. In 1972 the United Nations called for a ten-year ban on whaling, but the Japanese and Norwegians ignored it. George Deacon, author of *The Antarctic Circumpolar Ocean,* writes: "By then it was too late: the stock of whales had been reduced to something like a tenth of its former size, and by 1980, except for one Japanese and two Soviet factories catching Minke Whales, Antarctic whaling came to an end."[13]

The saddest aspect of Antarctic whaling, and the most telling about the exploitation of the ocean, was that it was clear to everyone who thought about it that the whales, and therefore the whaling industry, were in trouble even while whaling was increasing. One of the first groups to report trouble was the

Discovery Committee. The British government set up the committee, which established a laboratory in King Edward's Cove, opposite the Grytviken whaling platform. From 1925 to 1931 Discovery researchers examined 3,700 whales there, and 2,300 more on factory ships. To determine age the researchers looked at traces of past ovulation, scars, the number of ridges on the whales' baleen plates, and the laminations (one per year) in a "long, conical, horny plug" that is found in the ears of whales.[14]

The seasons of 1929–30 and 1930–31 were the whaling industry's best years, in terms of profit. Antarctic whalers produced 2.5 and 3.5 million barrels, respectively (6 barrels to a ton), and the whaling companies had dividends of 30 to 50 percent. They were not, however, the years of the greatest kill. The number of whales killed reached its highest point a bit later, in 1937–38. Whalers caught, killed, and processed close to 55,000 whales then, the most ever in a season, before or after. But the whales were smaller than during earlier seasons, that fact alone a sign that the industry and the whales were in trouble. In the banner years of 1929–30 and 1930–31 the take was 38,000 and 43,000.[15]

But as the whales declined, whaling expanded. Factory ships were being built. And they were using more and more whale catchers, fifteen, then eighteen, then twenty-four for a Soviet factory ship. Shore whaling gave way to the factory ships. In the 1930–31 season thirty-eight factory ships hunted the Antarctic waters. Most of them were small. And almost all of them called at South Georgia to go through customs and unload oil. "It was said that more ships passed through the customs at South Georgia in 1930–31 than entered the port of Liverpool in a comparable period."[16]

Like the sealers before them, the modern whalers left precious little description of the ocean itself. Few of them were given to literary pursuits, and it seems fair to say that the sea was not their interest, not an end in itself, not something to think about except in terms of their work. But they cannot have loved it much. Observers like Ommaney and Robertson, and Murphy before them, write of the whalers as men who suffered cruelty and inflicted it.

Surely there was little of the romantic love of nature that now brings tourists to South Georgia, or the love of knowledge that attracts scientists. Indeed, one passage from Robertson, writing in the 1950s, is a reminder of how recent the love of whales is. His book was printed in part in the *New Yorker,* not a magazine ever characterized by gross insensitivity to the moral issues of its time. He wrote approvingly of the captain's penchant for shooting killer whales, now known as orcas to most people, fixtures in both nature calendars and Sea World shows. And he described the scene of orcas feeding on the remains of the whales his ship was killing and processing. The orcas were eating the offal, the parts that even the factory couldn't use. "Only hyenas on land and vultures in the air can convey the same sense of remorseless ill-will against all creation that killer whales convey as they slowly approach their loathsome victuals."[17] There is no irony in the statement, no sense of any ill-will against creation on the part of the whaling industry or the captain with his high-powered rifle.

It is hard to imagine a greater transformation of any creature in the popular mind. *Free Willy* was a successful movie about a schoolboy releasing a captive orca. Today all whales are environmental emblems. Every schoolchild in America has been bombarded with the notion that whales are sentient, noble creatures, far more noble than ourselves. I found one of my daughters in tears one night when she was about eight. Many things might have prompted the tears—exhaustion, a new school, trouble with the rest of the family or friends. But what she said was that it was the fate of the planet. Human beings, she said, were killing all the world's creatures, polluting the land and the oceans. Usually a strong proponent of environmentalism, I felt I had to make the case for industry, for forestry, even for whaling in the past. We did it to live, I said. If we didn't use the earth's resources we would disappear from the face of the planet. Fine, she said. It would be better for the earth if all the human beings disappeared.

I was shocked, partly because she was depressed. Something had to be going on other than the degradation of the environment to make her so gloomy. But it was also clear that she was expressing her distress in the language of the times, that her sense of devil humanity as the scourge of the earth, perhaps even without a legitimate claim to its own survival, was part and parcel of the educated young person's Zeitgeist.

On my tourist cruise along the Antarctic peninsula, the passengers gloried in the penguins and flying birds, the several varieties of seals, and the sculptured ice. But the whales were the prize. And the sense of the ocean that they lived in was one of magic, of the holy wilderness.

It's typical for writers to be skeptics, to look for what is underneath the good causes, but with whales you don't even have to look. It's obvious. Loving whales is easy. Cost-free, like loving elephants. In the United States we no longer need, or even imagine that we need, the products we used to make from whales. The lubricating oils have been replaced by the products of the petrochemical industry, arguably doing more damage to the planet than whaling ever did. Other environmental causes are harder sells, as a biologist from the New England Aquarium, Scott Kraus, observed: "The public gets hung up on whaling, but what's really worse is what we flush down the toilet."[18]

Japan and Norway, the only nations currently whaling (although Iceland may follow suit soon) have become international pariahs for their actions, even though the main whale they want to hunt, the minke, is widespread, with an apparently healthy population. All population estimates for whales are questionable, but there may well be more than 750,000 in the Southern Ocean. Japan apparently kills about 600 a year. In the north, Norway claims there are more than 80,000 and that they kill about 300.

It has been suggested that whales need to be protected because of their intelligence. And yet, on the other side, proponents of whaling have pointed out that pigs are unusually intelligent. There are ethically consistent vegetarian environmentalists and animal defenders who oppose any human use of animals. But a public outcry against the worldwide production of spare ribs, pork chops, and bacon seems unlikely. Of course, whales are wild animals, but one Norwegian whaler was quoted in the *New York Times* as saying: "Killing a minke is no different than killing a deer."[19] As to the ecological arguments, scientists disagree. The IWC's own scientific advisory committee suggested allowing a limited hunt of minke whales, and the chairman of the committee resigned when the recommendations were ignored.

I had a chance to spend some time watching minke whales from the *Polar Sea* when I rejoined the ship after a month at McMurdo for a two-week oceanographic cruise around the Ross Sea. Two filmmakers for a British television program were onboard for the night and staying in my cabin. At about 11 P.M., when I had already gotten in bed and was falling asleep, readjusting to the ship's noises, they came down to pick up some camera equipment and told me there were whales off the stern. I dressed and went up on deck into broad daylight.

We were in McMurdo Sound. There was a pod of about six minke whales, lolling just off the stern in the open water. We were parked in the ice, not moving. Mount Erebus was lit by the sun behind clouds, and at the stern the whales moved smoothly, with a slowness that suggested sun and laziness. Some of the whales' backs were almost black, others close to bronze with greenish patches. Their bellies were white. Some of the dorsal fins curved more than others. One was missing its tip. Another was deeply notched. Their jaws were undershot, and the lower jaw came to a perfect hydrodynamic point. Their breathing was rhythmic, the exhaling not too loud, but noticeable as they blew air up from the nostril on top of their heads. When they inhaled, the nostrils opened, wet and dark.

Sometimes the whales moved in unison, sometimes they crossed one another's path, and sometimes they dived under the ice. At times we could see only one or two. Then all of them would emerge, rising and then sinking, and the surface of the water would give way to the syncopated off-rhythm tempo of their breathing, like a calm frenzy. One thing was abundantly clear. I couldn't kill one.

Gary Snyder's poem "Mother Earth: Her Whales" suggests the sort of emotions that must come over any modern observer of the creatures:

> The whales turn and glisten, plunge
>   and sound and rise again
> Hanging over subtly darkening deeps
> Flowing like breathing planets
>   in the sparkling whorls of living light—
>
> And Japan quibbles for words on
>   what kinds of whales they can kill?[20]

In the ship's library, there was a science fiction classic that I came on by accident, *The War with the Newts,* written by Karel Čapek, a Czech, in the 1920s. In it, huge intelligent newts are discovered in the South Seas and put into virtual slavery by humanity to build vast underwater structures and new islands. Then the newts, tired of being exploited, turn against humankind.

One passage suggested to me the rational arguments about whaling and whether a ban on killing the minkes is fair. The quotation comes at a point in the story when the newts and humanity are attempting to negotiate an agreement to avoid war. " 'A British gentleman,' declared the English Premier, speaking for the whole nation, 'protects animals, but he does not come to terms with them.' "[21]

In the spring of 1994 the International Whaling Commission voted to further protect whales by declaring a sanctuary for them in the waters around Antarctica. The group decided to ban whaling in an area that covers 8 million square miles. The vote was 23–1. Six nations abstained. Japan cast the negative vote. Norway did not attend the meeting.[22]

Chapter 8

WORKING THE WATER

When I was just beginning to think of a book on the Southern Ocean I went to Lamont Doherty Earth Observatory near my home in New York State. I talked to Arnold Gordon, an oceanographer whom one of his colleagues referred to, half joking, as the "king of the Southern Ocean." Gordon's work has concentrated on heat exchange in the Southern Ocean, particularly in the form of miles-long stretches of open water in the midst of sea ice, called polynyas. It is through these that the Southern Ocean seems to dump the heat it acquires from the other world oceans.

We discussed what shape the book might take, and Gordon lamented the focus of popular science books, magazine articles, and television shows on seals and whales and birds. What was seldom covered was physical and chemical oceanography, which produced insights into physical and chemical processes in the ocean, its currents and temperatures, its nutrients. He emphasized that the formation and disappearance of ice, the cycles of silicon and carbon uptake, the currents and the temperature gradients were of utmost importance to even a rudimentary understanding of the ocean.

I had, in fact, first looked for a spot on an oceanographic research vessel, although even some oceanographers warned me off them, since the cruises may consist of going back and forth over sections of open sea and tending to equipment and computers while the scientists onboard, who may get on a ship only once a year or once every few years, jockey for research time.

The oceanography of the Southern Ocean could—and does—fill many volumes. Oceanographers study, among other things, the temperature, salinity, and movement of water, what might be called the structure of the ocean. Most dramatic in the Southern Ocean is the movement south and east of so-called warm deep water that originates in the North Atlantic, and the northward flow of cold, fresh bottom water formed in the Antarctic. The cold Southern Ocean feeds the Humboldt Current along the west coast of South America, providing a wealth of minerals and nutrients to feed vast fish stocks off the coast and on to the Galapagos. The Southern Ocean also feeds cold and productive currents on the other coast of South America, and up the west coast of Africa.

I did, in the end, get to join an oceanographic cruise, although it was a brief one and involved mostly the maintenance and repair of research equipment. It was not so much a window on the ocean itself as it was a glimpse of the sort of tedious and difficult housekeeping that supports the scientific enterprise. At the end of my stay in Antarctica I left McMurdo and rejoined the *Polar Sea* for a two-week cruise around the Ross Sea. It was a glimpse not so much into the romance of science in remote places, but into the difficulties of such science. And it was a chance for me to begin to mull over my own relation to the Southern Ocean, to think about what it was, not to sealers or scientists or the Coast Guard, but to me.

I rejoined the *Polar Sea* on February 6 and watched an Arnold Schwarzenegger movie, *The Running Man.* There was a scientific contingent of five men, technicians and graduate students, and the two technicians who were in charge of the operation were Dave Mucciarone and Chris Moser. Mucciarone, muscular, quick-talking, given to a running commentary of everything he was doing, was from Rice University. He had a master's in geology and had done some work with oil companies before getting into oceanography. Chris Moser was quick-witted, bald, and a vegetarian. Not that any of these characteristics were linked. There was no vegetarian option in the officers' mess. Judging from the food on the icebreaker, long after the military has adjusted to openly gay soldiers and sailors, vegetarians will still feel ostracized. Moser also had a master's, his in oceanography.

The degree is significant in the academic hierarchy, the structure of science. It almost restricts you to a secondary research role, as a technician, for instance. By and large, only those with Ph.D.s move on to professorships and acquire their own grants, and thus direct the course of their own research. With a master's, you toil in the vineyards of others, usually. Mucciarone was working with a scientist from Rice, Rob Dunbar, and Moser's main work was designing sediment traps.

For some reason this cruise had a completely different character from the trip down. The scientific contingent seemed to have more fun with the Coast Guard; everybody seemed looser. The minor but clear tension that had been present on the way down seemed gone. These two weeks were frantic rather than tense. And I got to know Moser and Mucciarone better than I had most of the researchers on the trip down. It may have been that with departure for home in sight, with much of my work done, I was more able to relax. Perhaps I had the sense that now that I had left McMurdo I had once again given over control to the Coast Guard. I was onboard ship. Where it went, I went.

I asked both Mucciarone and Moser directly if being involved in science changed the way they looked at the ocean. "You have a scalpel and forceps," Mucciarone said. "You're cutting it up and looking inside." When you study what is going on chemically in the ocean, he said, you see how delicate the balance is, how easily it's disturbed. And the focus that a scientific project or scientific knowledge gives to your attention enhances rather than diminishes your appreciation of the ocean. He recalled going on vacation with his wife and getting so excited about the rocks they were seeing. "So somebody says of the mountain, 'How pretty.' I say, 'Look at that diorite sill.' "

Moser thought his work if anything helped him see the bigger picture, how the planet as a whole worked, and how the oceans fit in. "The oceans are a leading force in the planet's ability to buffer changes, absorbing carbon dioxide and other things. A lot of systems that have the potential of mediating perturbations in the environment are in the ocean. The oceans are kind of like our mother. They have the capacity to smooth things out. I'm still sort of awestruck by what the ocean is doing."

Moser was nominally the chief scientist for the trip, but he and Mucciarone seemed to share the planning. Nonetheless, a leader had to be named. As a military organization, the Coast Guard demanded hierarchy. Several researchers told me that the Coast Guard could not deal effectively with a group in which there was no designated leader and no fixed mission. If anything, the definition of the mission was more important than the anointing of a leader. Mission definition is a delicate process, one that would have entranced Machiavelli, because once an exercise is completed, the military must determine whether the mission was successful, whether its described goals were met. How you defined your mission at the start determined whether you succeeded in the end.

Our mission was fairly straightforward; we were going to pick up and replace sediment traps designed to document silica and carbon production in the Ross Sea. The traps were part of a research project that was designed to get information on the biological productivity of the Ross Sea. All living things produce carbon, and how much carbon is caught in a sediment trap documents biological production during a certain period of time. A certain kind of algae called diatoms produce skeletons of calcium or silica. In the Southern Ocean, which is low on calcium, the diatoms make silica skeletons. So silica deposits are another indication of life cycles of the small and unfamous.

The particular project we were servicing involved several scientists working together over a period of years. Their goal was to document—month by month—how much carbon and silica were produced at certain locations in the Ross Sea. The essential bit of equipment for this study was a sediment trap, consisting in its simplest form of a funnel leading into a tube. Set at a fixed location and depth, the tube would collect whatever fell into it. Not water. Water is the medium through which the plankton, remnants of plankton, and fecal pellets drift down, partially dissolving to enrich the deeper water and accumulating at the bottom. As this material drifts down through the water, the trap catches it, and the tube fills up.

The traps are about 8 feet tall, with a funnel top and fifteen sediment collecting tubes. The tubes were set into a rotating disk, a kind of lazy Susan dedicated to accumulating rather than dispensing organic matter. A battery-powered electric motor directed by a computer chip moved the disk, placing a tube under the funnel, leaving it there for a month to collect sediment, then moving the disk another notch to place the next tube under the funnel. The traps are also equipped with current meters, to record water movement.

A mooring—the whole set of anchors, traps, line, and communications devices in one location—consisted of an anchor at the bottom, equipped with an acoustic release; a sediment trap; and a line extending up to another sediment trap at 200 meters with a group of plastic floats just above it.

We were to retrieve three moorings of this sort. The technicians would first call the traps with a sonar transponder, which sends coded sound pulses through the water and listens for a return signal. Once the technicians on the icebreaker had established the rough location of the mooring, one of them would go out in a work boat with the Coasties, get as close to directly over the trap as he could, and then send a signal to trip the acoustic release. The whole array would then float up to the surface. The small boat would snatch the floats, pull them to the breaker, and then hand over the line so that the whole mooring could be hauled up by winch and crane.

The first morning back on the ship there was a mission planning meeting. It was the poor man's version of a space shot. The logistics of retrieving the moorings were planned down to the last step—who would grab this part, where the J-frame (crane) and the snatch block would swing, when to release current meters, who to have on deck, how many people were needed and where they should be stationed. I found it hard to stay awake. They even decided on which knots to use—figure eights. As I fought to stay awake, I wondered what a joumard was.

This cruise was unusual in one unfortunate way. Moser's company had discovered, after the sediment traps had been dropped the season past, that it had made a mistake in programming the computer chip that told the lazy Susan when to move. The Oregon-based company had provided traps for research programs in the North Pacific, which could be checked more frequently than those in the Antarctic. When Moser and others suspected the error, they pulled those traps up and found that indeed the systems were not working properly.

The traps drew the power to run the computer and move the disk from a battery, which did not have enough energy to keep the computer on for a whole year. So the program written to run the trap directed the computer to wake up every eight and a half minutes and consult with a calendar to find out if it was time to do something, like move the sediment-collecting tubes along.

The problem was with the way the computer consulted its calendar. It counted time—in hundredths of seconds—from January 1, 1980 (an arbitrary date). Each time the computer woke up, the program told it to add 512 seconds to the number of seconds that had elapsed in the last decade or so. However, the mathematics were set up so that there was a maximum number that could be handled in this calculation. After the first two tubes were rotated, an overflow of numbers stopped the progress of the program and left the computer on, draining the battery. In the traps in the Pacific the program had stopped after the first two tubes were rotated. In about a day and a half after that, the computer ran the battery down, and that was the end of it. The tubes stopped moving under the funnel.

In traps located in the Pacific, a few hundred miles from the Oregon coast, the problem could be solved by replacing the traps. These traps in the Ross Sea, however, could only be reached once a year. If the same thing had happened here, the researchers would have lost a year's worth of data. It's a risky business, oceanography of this sort. You spend the time and money to design a project, to get the equipment built, to test it. You get the grant money to get down to Antarctica. You successfully manage to put your traps in the Ross Sea, despite whatever weather and ice conditions might interfere with that process, and then one slip, one glitch, and a year's data are lost.

The first place we tried to pick up a trap was Granite Harbor, straight north of the Ross Ice Shelf between Beaufort and Franklin Islands. Starting at 7 P.M. Mucciarone dragged a hydrophone over the side to talk to the mooring, using its replies to measure the distance to it from more than one point, thus triangulating it, fixing an approximate location. Each mooring had two acoustic releases, a primary and a backup, and each had nicknames, one male and one female. So as Mucciarone sent the signals through the hydrophone and received answers he also talked to himself as if he were having an actual conversation with them, urging them to respond, to hear the signal, not to have a dead acoustic release (with separate power) as well as a dead computer. The first two were Paul and Carey. He spoke to them as someone shooting craps might talk to his dice.

Once the location was fixed, two small boats were lowered over the side. Mucciarone went out in an inflatable boat with a couple of Coasties, and another group was in a 25-foot wooden boat. The weather was cold, about 13 degrees. The sky was gray, the wind was blowing, and it was snowing. The first part of the mooring didn't come on deck until about 11 P.M., four hours after the operation started. We saw at once that the trap had failed. Two sediment tubes were partly full and the third was overflowing; the tubes had stopped rotating after two movements.

The trap looked like big reddish brown fiberglass hourglasses or egg timers. With the top of the hourglass full of seawater as the crewmen hoisted it from the water, it weighed 800 pounds. By the time the boats brought in the second trap the sun was out from behind clouds, the wind was down, and it was warming up. The sea was pacific, like Oliver Wendell Holmes's purring cat. It was 1 A.M.

In one sense the operation had been successful; Mucciarone et al. had retrieved the two current meters and the two sediment traps. Both traps had failed as predicted; nonetheless, the researchers were relieved and pleased to get the equipment back. Some information could still be drawn from the sediment that had been accumulated and from the current meter. The chips would be reprogrammed, the sediment traps redeployed, and the following season, presumably, a full year's data would be recovered.

There was not universal satisfaction, however. The effort had been prolonged and awkward. Lieutenant Jorge Arroyo, the operations officer, known as Ops, was the man in charge of the logistics of the operation. When I spoke to him after the traps were finally in, I said, "Success!" He said, "Some people might call it that." Perhaps five hours seemed like a long stretch to him to get two sediment traps onboard.

There were a couple of reasons for the agonizing effort to retrieve the traps. First, the crew was not used to this sort of mission. In fact, the crew was hardly used to the icebreaker itself. At the beginning of the cruise, when the icebreaker left Seattle, 60 percent of the crew was new to the ship, some just out of boot camp.

And if the crew was green, the icebreaker was not set up for oceanography. On a research ship the entire fantail would be set up for deploying and retrieving instruments, and the deck would be near water level to make it easier to get the instruments onboard. The icebreaker, in contrast, had a very small casting deck on the port side, where the traps had to be retrieved and later deployed.

Once the trap was onboard the research team began a new regimen, removing, cleaning, and replacing the tubes; storing the sediment; resetting the current meters; reprogramming the faulty calendar instructions in the computer chip. The tubes had to be filled with formalin mixed with seawater that had been gathered and filtered at Mactown. The chemical would kill organisms as they fell into the tube. Otherwise they would keep growing, and the point of the experiment was to document what fell into the trap, not what grew in them. The mix is denser than seawater so it does not float out.

Back in Texas, researchers would filter and dry the sediment, then put samples in a foil capsule for analysis by gas chromatography. In a small furnace the sediment would be ignited at very high heat so that it burned in a flash. Detectors in the furnace would record which gases were produced in what amounts.

We recovered another mooring with its two traps at another

spot. The operation went a bit more quickly even though the sea was running a small swell, which made bringing the trap onto the ship difficult. At one minute, the cable from the crane was slack, as the 800-pound trap floated at the top of the swell. The next minute, at the trough of the swell, the cable snapped taut; the trap cleared the water and swung in the air. Some of the young Coasties out in the inflatable and the wooden boats got seasick because of the swell, and one fell in the water as the wooden boat was being hauled up onto the ship. After a warm shower he was none the worse for his dunk.

One night, when things were otherwise quiet, I watched Geoff Pierson, a graduate student from the North Carolina State University who had a small part in the cruise, take a crack at his own project, which was to deploy an acoustic mapping device. It was a small catamaran, with a plate through which sounds are sent, and a long array of hydrophones—called an eel—designed to pick up the echo. What was supposed to happen was that the sounds would be projected from the plate, and the eel would pick up the echo and convey the signals to a computer and printer onboard to produce a map of the bottom. It didn't work, which made me think that the remarkable thing about scientific research to me is not that the researchers are so brilliant and the experiments so precise and elegant, but that scientists have such extraordinary determination, such tolerance for frustration and difficulty.

In this sense television has been a mixed blessing for science. Documentaries have popularized the studies of the oceans, the heavens, the earth and its inhabitants, the battle against disease, all the ways in which scientists try to pry loose the secrets of material existence. But television cannot tolerate tedium. It can only tolerate excitement. I think viewers who watch "Nova," for instance, must often feel that they missed something when they were in high school, because science seemed so difficult in the most annoying ways—the chemistry experiments that wouldn't come out right, the Bunsen burners getting too hot, the results not fitting the textbook. And they imagine that those who continued in science were the ones who tricked out a secret from the process, who found the true path around the boredom. There is some truth to that idea, I suppose. You have to have the right kind of intellect to see the point, to determine the pattern and meaning in the number. But perhaps as important to those who went on in science is that they just kept at it.

Certainly scientists see the beauty in their results. They have a sense of the wonder of nature, of the patterns and secrets they can tease out from the sludge of experience. But, although it is always tricky for an observer who gets to see only bits and snatches of scientific work to draw larger conclusions, it seems that most of a researcher's time is spent knee-deep in that sludge, literally and figuratively. Scientific findings may, in the end, be lovely, clean, and precise, but the process by which they are achieved is messy.

On this particular night, Pierson fiddled with the dials (a layman's impression) for a couple of hours and then reeled his apparatus in. Noise was swamping the signals he was trying to read. The noise could have been coming from the ship, or from the equipment itself. It may not have been riding properly. If it was bouncing around in the propwash, that would affect its performance too.

On the next day he tried again. As he set the sled out, the sun was behind the clouds threatening to set. The clouds near the horizon alternated pale shades of gray, blue, white, and pink. Two snow petrels flew by like doves, visible against the darker clouds and swooping like pigeons. They seemed to me like descending grace, the images of the Holy Spirit, one member of the Trinity. An old bluegrass song came to mind: "On the wings of a snow white dove / He sends His pure, sweet Love / He sends us His love / On the wings of a dove."

Here were two impressions of the Southern Ocean, two

images deeply set in their frameworks of knowledge. In one a graduate student was struggling to use sound waves to produce an image of the ocean floor. He was as thoroughly involved in practical, technical thinking as one could be. Like a hunter pursuing dinner he concentrated on signals and signs, his prey numbers, data, information—a map of a part of the planet that we hadn't had before. His work may not have been the most glamorous or important or successful research done that season in the Antarctic, but it was a representative part of the whole scientific enterprise. His research, and that of scientists in all disciplines, from cartography to acoustics, rests on a structure of understanding, an accumulated body of evidence, that gives meaning to the squiggles on paper that his apparatus produced.

I am probably more aware than many nonscientists of how acoustic imaging works, of how bouncing sound waves off an object can produce a picture. Still, my understanding is shallow, not deep. I take a great deal at the word of the scientists. The information and understanding they achieve comes to me secondhand. The image of the snow petrels descending like the grace of God came to me in a different way.

I am not a believer, but I am thoroughly steeped in the imagery of Christianity, of Roman Catholicism, from my upbringing. I can no more free myself of the sense of the divine in nature, of the images that come to me, of the meaning that sunsets and birds and light have than I can cut myself loose from the English language. I may have been able to glimpse Pierson's ocean and Moser's ocean, in the way I read or listen to French, in translation. (I get along but I am not truly bilingual.) But in thinking about it, it seemed clear that my ocean was a different one.

In my deepest self I may be not just a lapsed Catholic, but a lapsed Platonist. "Plato was wrong: what is is absolute. Ideas pale." That is what I say, what I argue, what I insist upon in my presentation of the data to fuzzy-thinking romantics and believers. But certainly I am arguing with myself as much as with anyone else. Ideas are what drive me. It was unclear whether it was the snow petrels, real and flying, or some Platonic image of them, some idea of what they might be or mean, that caused something in me to sing when I saw them, to reverberate—perhaps with naturally evolved biophilia—but certainly with hope and longing.

We had retrieved two moorings but were not able to reach the third. Mucciarone called and called, but it did not answer. The weather was turning bad, so we went back to the first two sites to redeploy the traps. After that, with luck, we would return and make one more attempt at recovering the third mooring.

First we set out the refurbished moorings at their previous locations. I went out in the MSB, the motor surf boat, to reset one of the moorings. As the boat was lowered from the icebreaker we held on to ropes dangling from the davits, descending hand over hand like ninjas, keeping our feet in the boat. This was a safety measure. If the boat somehow fell away from us, if the lowering went awry, we would hang on the ropes and make our way back up the hull. When we came back to the boat we followed the reverse procedure.

Once successfully in the water we towed the top end of the array away from the ship. The technicians dropped first the floats, which would rest under the surface, then the first sediment trap into the water. After we had towed these far enough away from the ship to prevent tangles, the group onboard would drop the second sediment trap and, at last, the anchor, 1,500 pounds of concrete blocks in a metal cage. We would then release our end and let the anchor pull the whole setup down.

The boat we were in was 25 feet long, shaped like a whale boat, self-bailing and self-righting. The boat is designed for rescue but it is the only one on the *Polar Sea* that can be put over with even a small chop. The bigger Arctic survey boat, at 13 tons, is too heavy to bang against the hull as the swell rises and falls.

A chief petty officer, Gary Van Allard, drove the boat. He was the man who had snagged the lost trash can. He was probably in his late twenties, with a rough, workingman's military attitude and a constant level of almost exuberant anger and profanity in the way he bossed the men—boys actually—under him. They seemed competent enough for their ages. As for Van Allard—everyone called him by his last name—watching him in action, you would have to conclude that competence was his religion.

This was the first time I was out on the water in the whole trip. I had seen the ocean only from the deck of the icebreaker—remote viewing. It was relatively calm, with just a wind chop, and we were near the icebreaker. I sensed no threat in the sea. The snow petrels were in the air again, five or six of them, along with a sooty albatross, the first albatross I'd seen since arriving at McMurdo a month ago.

The sea was dark. I was unable to tease a color out of it. I suppose it had to be some color, a deep bluish gray, but I didn't see it. What I really saw looking at the surface was a shifting pattern of light and dark, each perturbation of the water producing different spots of shadow and glare. The same water, when you looked through it from the submerged portion of an iceberg, would be aquamarine, a suitable name.

The sky was overcast, with purple and lavender clouds, and above them fluffier gray and whitish clouds and a bright blue sky, cerulean. The sky, the sea—both were unreadable. Without whales or birds to meld the worlds of air and water, to make them interact, there are only surfaces. No religious symbols; the unyielding and impenetrable texture and pattern of modernism. Was this enough, I wondered, to bring back from my trip? Wasn't it my business, like the scientists', to breach surfaces, whether with fishing line, acoustic array, sediment trap, or literary analysis? Or ought I simply to receive and report the surface? There is a story of the novelist and playwright Samuel Beckett, author of *Waiting for Godot,* returning to hearth and home after a hard day's work writing. His wife is supposed to have said to him as he said hello and kissed her, "No meaning again today, dear?"

Meaning or not, messing about in boats is, of course, superb fun. I loved being out at sea, had no hint of seasickness, enjoyed the chop and roll in the boat, was sorry to return to the ship.

On February 12 the roll on the icebreaker was a mere 5 degrees, this out of a maximum 90 degrees. It was minimal, but you swayed when you walked, and in the wardroom the coffee spilled out of the coffeemaker. I could not imagine what a 50-degree roll would be like. How would I get to the bridge, or go to sleep, or take notes? The seas were running at 10 feet. This didn't seem like much from the deck of the *Polar Sea,* but nobody seemed to want to take the boat out for another redeployment. The wind was about 20 knots. I wanted to go for another boat ride, to see what it was like out there. I mentioned this to Van Allard. His response was succinct and clear. "Fuck no, no fucking way."

Our last effort was to look for the array of two traps that we had not found before. The two acoustic releases were Marian and Richard. There was another release at Granite Harbor, lost a few seasons ago, that we had briefly listened for on the off chance of finding it when the weather had forced us away from Marian and Richard. That setup had only a single release, Tony. When Mucciarone came back to the ship after trying unsuccessfully to find that mooring, he said, "Tony, he sleeps with the fishes."

Before we went out with Van Allard in the MSB, Mucciarone contacted Marian from the icebreaker. "That's her," he said, "she's awake." But by the time we got out in the boat the releases were not responding properly. We went back and forth looking for a good signal. When Mucciarone finally found Marian again and tried to trigger a release, there was no response.

We spent three hours trying to call Marian. We called Richard. He never answered at all. The sun was bright. The Transantarctic Mountains in the distance cut the sky so sharply that a ridge of peaks looked like a flint knife with a scalloped edge. I was putting the hydrophone in the water and pulling it out, so my hands gradually got wetter and colder. The air temperature was in the 20s. The wind chop made the water sloppy, and the boat was going up and down maybe 10 feet.

As time went by Mucciarone swore at Marian. Van Allard swore at Marian. Everyone in the boat swore at something. Cold hands and weariness, the relentless movement of the boat and the water, and the growing disgruntlement of everyone in the boat gradually obscured any thoughts except the desire to return to the icebreaker. The sludge of experience, the overwhelming weight of the mundane, had sunk both the effort to get the mooring and any effort of mine to think of anything beyond physical discomfort. Sometimes, in the presence of unpleasant actuality, the consciousness that takes the place of imagination is an exceedingly narrow one, of pain, discomfort, seasickness. There are no atheists in foxholes and no philosophers in small boats when the sea is rough. We never did get the mooring.

Chapter 9

THE OCEAN

One of the most common superlatives attached to the Southern Ocean is "stormiest." If not universally accepted as the stormiest ocean on earth (some would claim the North Atlantic), it is certainly in the running. And if the term "Southern Ocean" falls strangely on most ears, "Cape Horn" is much more familiar, because the difficulty and struggle of rounding the Horn is the stuff of history and romance.

The accounts of rounding the Horn are numerous. One such, typical enough, is found in *A Voyage Around the World*, by George Anson, published in 1748. He describes the extreme rolling of the ship and its dangers:

> And though we were extremely careful to secure ourselves from these shocks, by grasping some fixed body, yet many of our people were forced from their hold, some of whom were killed, and others greatly injured; in particular, one of our best seamen was canted over-board and drowned, another dislocated his neck, a

> third was thrown into the main-hold and broke his thigh, and one of our Boatswain's Mates broke his collar-bone twice; not to mention many other accidents of the same kind.[1]

The exploits of the Cape Horn sailing ships that tackled the Drake Passage in the 1840s are famous. Some clipper ships made the passage to San Francisco in under one hundred days. Others took almost that long in the Drake Passage, trying to round the Horn. The *Golden Eagle* spent eighty-eight days, with fifteen crewmen injured, the *East Indian* ninety-four days.

The Cape Horn ship, says Allan Villiers, "was a wind-driven sea vehicle of beauty and, at her best, of astonishing efficiency—the most splendid blend of utility and sea strength and functional beauty ever achieved by European man."[2] And, yet, with that presumed efficiency and beauty, the ships and men were lost with appalling frequency.

Villiers, who was master of the *Joseph Conrad,* the last full-rigged ship to round Cape Horn (in 1935), investigated the winter of 1905, past the time of clipper ship races but when men were still battling the Horn. In ships' logs he found that thirty-three masters had died, some of natural causes, as had five masters' wives and sixty-nine apprentices. No one seemed to take much care about the reported cause of death. For instance, he writes: "'Dropsy' is a strong favorite in the 'cause of death' columns, but one is forced to conclude that its meaning, if any, is that the deceased had dropped dead." He continues:

> the only persons aboard who were invariably free of symptoms of senility and never seemed to die from "dropsy" were the apprentices, but the casualty rate among these could be appalling. They were tossed out of the rigging or washed overboard and left behind in what seems almost a careless profusion.[3]

As to the weather they faced, Villiers quotes one captain's advice: "You'll get no sleep. You'll get so wet so long your skin will come off with your socks, if you get time to take them off.

But with luck, you'll get past Cape Horn and, by the grace of God, you won't kill anybody."[4]

Today, the Southern Ocean is still known for the challenge it poses to ships, and sailing ships still test it in the Whitbred 'Round the World Race and on individual cruises. W. A. Robinson, who wrote of his 1952 voyage from Tahiti to Chile and then the Galapagos and back to Tahiti, described weather he encountered in his 70-foot yacht when he was far south in the latitudes known as the Roaring Forties and roughly halfway from Tahiti to South America.[5]

Robinson described the storm as "the ultimate conditions I had never yet encountered," and he had sailed everywhere.

> It is banal to use the term "hurricane" as it is so misused, particularly in the accounts of sailing craft. But I have experienced several recorded hurricanes in my life, both on land and at sea, and this was worse than any of them. Before the wind had reached its peak there had been a whole new set of shrieks and howls in the rigging and fittings. I now learned something entirely new; that when the wind exceeds a certain point most of these noises stop, and this was more ominous than ever . . .
>
> When I spoke of the culminating experience of a life of voyaging, this is what I had in mind. When a fifty-ton, seventy-foot vessel surfboards shudderingly down the face of a great sea on its breaking crest, you have experienced something. At these times she was going downhill at such a steep angle that when she reached the bottom she would bury her bowsprit before rising.[6]

In his appendix for sailors Robinson estimates that the waves during the storm reached 50 feet high, and the wind speed was 100 miles per hour.

The size and nature of waves in the Southern Ocean has been a matter of much dispute and discussion. Cook described "prodigious high seas." Dumont d'Urville reported a wave of 100 feet off the Cape of Good Hope. William Scoresby described waves 43 feet high. The scientific survey ship *Discovery*, using a wave recorder, got significant wave heights of 30 feet on some occasions and maximums of 60–70 feet.

The original notion was that the waves had the entire circumference of the globe to build up height. Deacon, in *The Antarctic Circumpolar Ocean*, claims this is not so. Wind and waves do not travel uninterrupted around the world toward the east. The wind changes, coming from the northwest as bad weather approaches and from the southwest as it passes. And the waves go with the wind.[7]

Rachel Carson, in *The Sea Around Us*, notes one fairly reputable claim of extreme wave height. The report, which Robinson notes as well, skeptically, was from the U.S.S. *Ramapo*.[8] It was going from Manila to San Diego in 1933. On February 6 the ship encountered 68-knot winds in gusts and squalls. The ship was in a trough when an officer on the bridge saw the sea rise to a level above an iron strap on the crow's nest on the mainmast. That strap was at 112 feet.

Other reports include those of the Soviets, of maximum height of waves in storms of 80–100 feet. In 1978 a U.S. satellite measured surface roughness and came up with data that showed waves of 33–36 feet somewhere in the ocean every few days. It seems to be accepted that the Southern Ocean has the longest waves and the widest, because of the strong winds and the great expanses that they travel. But enormously high waves in height have been described elsewhere.

In 1944 the British Admiralty Research Laboratory calculated how waves travel. They discovered that a swell from a storm near Cape Horn traveled 7,000 miles in nine days. It reached the coast of England at "the diminished height of 12 inches."[9]

We left Mactown on February 17. My strongest wish, except to return home, was to experience a storm, a tremendous, impressive, frightening storm. With the fool's faith in technology I had complete confidence in the safety of the *Polar Sea*.

Occasionally I felt that this was a mere dilettante's desire for excitement, not shared by true sailors. When I was in college the more severely radical leftists referred to students who marched and shouted and played Rolling Stones records about fighting in the streets as "middle class adventurers." I wondered if this was who I was on the icebreaker as well—doomed to go through life as a middle-class adventurer.

But although no one else on the *Polar Sea* ever admitted to any desire to experience a great storm, once I returned home I did find proof that real sailors may in fact harbor secret hopes for serious weather. Robinson wrote of his ultimate storm: "Again and again that night, I asked myself why I was there—and had no better answer than that perhaps this was the very thing that had drawn me into this voyage, an unexpressed urge to experience a real Cape Horn gale."[10]

On this, the last leg of my trip, the oceanographers were gone. Willie Weeks and Martin Jeffries were back. And the ship was also carrying about thirty men and women as passengers. Most were civilian workers from McMurdo. Two were navy personnel. Flights to New Zealand on the navy Hercs were always tight at the end of the season. And the icebreaker was headed to a port that attracted travelers, Valparaiso, Chile. For anyone with time, here was a chance to cross the Pacific at a leisurely pace, to experience the slow transition from ice to warmth, from darkness, which was coming fast to Antarctica, to light.

McMurdo was hunkering down, compressing. There would be only one bar open in the long dark for the few hundred people overwintering. The folks who were staying were as excited as those who were leaving. I realized that I had absolutely no desire ever to spend a winter in Antarctica. I was not in the least bit sad to leave. I had no plans to return. I was delighted to be putting out to sea. And I was determined to make this my weather trip. I would watch the waves and the swells, I would frequent the weather station, I would track the winds and currents.

On the evening of our departure I was on the bridge as we passed Franklin Island off the port bow. A hint of twilight and color was in the sky, pale pinks and lavenders along with blues, whites, and pearl colors, bluish grays. There were icebergs ahead and on the horizon, no swell, and a little wind chop. There was a rosy glow off to starboard, and sometimes a far bit of ice caught the light and seemed to glow.

South and west of us, astern, puffy cumulus clouds ran down the slanted vault of the sky, with other horizontal clouds lit up behind them and a red glow at horizon. The feeling of heading out to sea, of moving, was satisfying beyond description. The openness of McMurdo, the enormous space compared to that of the *Polar Sea*, was in truth claustrophobic. The claustrophobia of the ship was in fact a disguise, a thin translucent wall beyond which lay the greatest openness possible on the surface of the earth.

We experienced February 18 twice. The first time we had this date, I drove the ship. Lieutenant Junior Grade Sef Shaw got permission for me to relieve the helmsman. Naturally there was no ice in sight. I drove straight ahead with my eye on the compass and the gauge that indicated the rudder movement. I tried to keep the course on true and to keep rudder changes within 5 degrees of the proper compass setting. I was so intent on my purpose I didn't look at the sea at all. I imagined doing this on a night watch, when it was dark and quiet.

According to the meteorology office the winds were at 6 knots and the boat speed was 15 knots. The crewmen in the office were teaching me how to calculate real wind speed and direction. Course 025 (the compass reading; 0 is due north and 180 is due south), wind direction relative to ship is 090, wind speed reading 6 knots, boat speed 15 knots—what was the real wind speed? Either you could sit down with pencil and paper and use trigonometry, or you could use the wonder wheel, a little plastic device with several circles. Of course, there are calculators that can do the trick as well. In any case the answer was 22 knots. As to sea state, the waves were 3 feet, swell 6 feet.

This was the most difficult observation for me to make, to see the difference between the waves and the swell, and to judge their heights. The swell is the movement of the water that is created over hundreds or thousands of miles by wind and storm. It is the baseline movement of the sea. Waves are the result of local wind conditions. The waves and the swells may well be moving in different directions. In fact, if they weren't, I couldn't imagine telling them apart. To me, the surface of the sea was still unreadable, but I was trying, under instruction, to decipher the puzzle.

The next day was also February 18. We had to have two of them to make up for the day we lost when we crossed the International Date Line the other way. The ship had crossed it November 19; I had crossed it in the air on December 14. On the second February 18 we pulled a weather station, one of Chuck Stearns's gadgets, off Scott Island. As the helicopter was flying a new one to the island on a sling load, the station fell into the sea. One of four lines of the pendant came loose. A few seconds later the station fell off into the water.

Some of the officers were joking about the accident, and one of the other pilots hushed them up as I approached. Suddenly nobody was talking at all. I wondered if the silence was for my benefit, if the officers worried that the dropped weather station would be a chapter in the book, complete with name, rank, and serial number of the pilot who dropped it. I would think the silence would be worse than the razzing. On a baseball team when someone is in a slump, he is always razzed. If the other players were silent and avoided the subject it would be worse, as if he really was dying, as if it was the end, not something that happens to everyone once in a while. On the other hand, maybe they don't razz him when reporters are in the clubhouse.

As we left Scott Island we changed course, and the ship started to roll. The seas were coming diagonally across the starboard bow, and the ship was rolling up to 20 degrees. I couldn't sleep. The mattress slid back and forth. Mops and buckets went bump in the night. My roommates' packs (I was with two lieutenants again, this time from the U.S. Navy) slid across the floor. Finally I stuffed a blanket next to the mattress to jam it tight in the bunk. About 4 A.M. I fell asleep. I was not seasick; I was sea-annoyed. Soon everyone else was annoyed too. At 5 P.M. in the wardroom, during dinner the next day, there was an announcement from the captain over the public address system that we had been ordered to return to McMurdo. The Ross Ice Shelf had begun calving, and the cargo ship *Green Wave* was trapped in Winter Quarters Bay by tabular icebergs.

I hadn't quite realized how intent I was on getting home until the possibility arose of a serious delay. The rumors were that the ship might then go straight to Puerto Vallarta instead of stopping in Valparaiso and thus not reach land until March 22, long after I was due home.

That night I was on deck in the gathering twilight. We had reached the time of year when the sun was flirting with setting, when there was a bit of both light and dark at McMurdo and environs. I saw people in the ice for the first time. The surface of the sea was a mix of water, large floes, grease ice, and pancake ice. I saw a canoe. The shadows on a bergy bit had produced the clear, unmistakable outline of one man in a canoe, paddling with a lot of gear. It looked as if he was going to have a tough trip. One bird was visible, a snow petrel probably, from the way it flew, but shadowy, less clear, less real than the momentary vision of the man in the canoe.

Now all the talk in the wardroom lounge turned to search and rescue cases. There was news of an old sailor with heart problems who had left Hawaii headed for Punta Arenas and was now nowhere to be found. Also, there was a boat from the Whitbred Race that seemed to be in trouble. Plus there was a tourist ship, the *Frontier Spirit,* going into Mactown in two weeks or so. Everyone was speculating about what sort of emergency might arise that could result in us being called back a second time for search and rescue. The talk was a festival of gloom, a morbid recounting of everything that could go wrong, of how we might never get home, both to torment landlubbers like me and, perhaps, to ward off really bad luck. Imagine the worst and it wouldn't come.

At this moment I lost all sympathy for tourism in the Antarctic. Up until then my position had been that tourists had as much right to experience the Antarctic as scientists did. I had not taken seriously the moaning and groaning by the NSF about having to rescue people who got in trouble. But the possibility, however remote, of me having to go back two more times to Mactown, perhaps even miss the birth of my baby, produced a surge of selfishness. Let them eat olives in Provence! Why did they need to come down to the ice?

It's easy enough to say that the tourists should be responsible for themselves. But that's simply not the way it works. The United States is the biggest presence in the Antarctic. Most of the tourists are U.S. citizens. From the Adirondack Mountains in New York, to Alaska, to Antarctica, when travelers are lost or stranded or in danger, rescue organizations, whether volunteer or official, spend the money and risk the welfare of their people to find and help travelers in trouble. At sea, any ship that can aid another in trouble must do so, the Coast Guard above all.

I was ready to ban tourism completely. Home had been becoming a more palpable presence ever since we'd left McMurdo. To be turned away from that goal, even though it was a trivial delay in the grand scheme of things, was infuriating. The executive officer reminded all of us to keep in mind the motto of Deep Freeze '83—the name of the southern cruise to Antarctica that year. It was taken from the movie *Meatballs*, and it was Bill Murray's advice to his counselors: "It just doesn't matter. It just doesn't matter."

Two days later the public address system crackled again and

the captain's voice asked for our attention. The *Green Wave* had gotten out. We were turning around, away from Mactown, toward Valpo, out of the fog, back toward home. There were cheers all over the ship.

On the twenty-second we passed an iceberg known as B-6, which was missing on the last ice chart from the National Oceanic and Atmospheric Administration. It had first been seen more than a month ago, and it had since moved 100 miles. B-6 covered 375 square miles, 15 by 25 nautical miles. It was many times the size of Manhattan. We picked it up on the radar first and altered our course slightly to get a look at it. It looked like the ice shelf itself.

The twenty-third was pizza night again. This time we were leaving the ice instead of entering it. The civilians were making the pizza this time, so I was down helping make everything from heavy cheese to ham and pineapple, an Australian favorite. As we were working the captain and XO come down. The captain said: "Whatever you're doing you're doing something right. We just left the ice." The ship's log showed that we stood in open water at 1955 hours at latitude 66 degrees 50.4 minutes, longitude 148 degrees 1.4 minutes.

The change in feeling from ice to open water was dramatic. We were now making time. Literally. When you're caught in ice and fog, time weighs on you. You look for ways to kill time. Now we were in control. Each minute, each second as the ship's props thrust us through the water we made time at a speed of 17 knots.

Though we had left pack ice we still saw bergs, some on the horizon, some near, some tabular, others carved. One was roughly semicircular, and one wing of it, one prominence, was like the sail of pelycosaur, but smooth, with no lines, and faintly blue. The rest of the berg faded in color from the dull white of fine china, to pearl gray in shaded areas, to the palest bluest blues. The berg seemed to have its own light, like a semiprecious stone.

I took to playing the cloud game with icebergs. I found a mountain range, the rock of Gibraltar, mesas, the recumbent sarcophagus of Tutankhamen, ventifact curves and whorls. Hydrofacts. We crossed the Antarctic Circle, 60 degrees south, during *Bill and Ted's Excellent Adventure*, one of many shipboard classics.

What came next is what I think of as the Big Sleep, a lassitude so heavy and unshakeable that I felt hypnotized. And I was not alone. From morning until night, day after day, the sea was calm and the ship held course on automatic pilot, following a great circle route at about 17 knots. Martin Jeffries and I would discuss our day's agenda after breakfast—naps, reading, naps. The trip was essentially over for both of us. I was hoping for a storm and a clear view of the Southern Cross, but that was all. We read. We walked around the ship. I took naps morning and afternoon in my bunk. I would come upon Martin in the officers' lounge, *The Last Lion* on his lap, napping.

One night we had a star lesson on deck, looking at the Southern Cross and an upside down Orion with red Betelgeuse and blue Rigel. Cygnus was the brightest. Mars and Jupiter were visible. The moon was nearly full, but waning. The crew was working, of course, but the passengers were sinking deep into the narcotic effect of steady movement over water and changing time zones. We traveled through something like one time zone a day. People were up at all hours and sleeping during the day if they had the opportunity. At breakfast some of us debated about whether it was too early to go back to bed.

It was clear, finally, by the time I was sitting on deck in a T-shirt in the sun, worrying about getting sunburned, that there was going to be no weather for me to write about. We had had a day or two of 20-degree rolls, but no storms. Apparently I had been the opposite of a Jonah. I brought good weather—bad for the book but a great recommendation if I wanted to travel onboard ship again. I had spent two months on the *Polar Sea* in the stormiest ocean on earth. We had traversed the entire Pacific, going through the Roaring Forties and the Furious Fifties twice. Not once had we seen the weather I saw crossing the Drake Passage on my first trip, 20- to 30-foot swells, and that wasn't a pleasant day for the Southern Ocean.

Soon the trip would end. I would land at Valparaiso, spend a day or two in Santiago, and fly home to my wife, my children, the birth of a new child, a book to write. I could no longer concentrate on taking notes. My journal became sparse and eventually blank. Trying not to think of home was like trying not to think of an elephant—an impossible task. And yet the ship had a hold on me. The suspension of life that occurs onboard ship is addictive. At sea you are always in transit, in transition. Nothing is fixed. Everything is immanent. A storm could come. A whale could break the surface. The future could hold anything.

My final memory of my voyage is of this stretch, when the land was pulling me back into schedules, work, and conventional time: In the sun, nearing South America, but still in the open ocean, I am standing on the quarter deck, watching the water. A wandering albatross is gliding. Then there are three together. They are a kite maker's dream, riding easily, dipping and gliding, flying with wings perpendicular to the surface. Feeling the breeze, watching the albatrosses, I am content. This is the ocean, as far as it will reveal itself: the bow wave of a ship, the swell, the birds, and the wind.

NOTES

Chapter 1: The Ocean

1. Joyce Carol Oates, "Against Nature," in *On Nature,* edited by Daniel Joseph Halpern (San Francisco: North Point Press, 1987).
2. John Hollander, "Adam's Task," in *We Animals,* edited by Nadya Aisenberg (San Francisco: Sierra Club Books, 1989).
3. "The Greenland Whale Fisheries," traditional.
4. Sanford Moss, *Natural History of the Antarctic Peninsula* (New York: Columbia University Press, 1988), p. ix.
5. F. A. Worsley, *Shackleton's Boat Journey* (New York: Norton, 1987).
6. W. Nigel Bonner, "Antarctic Science and Conservation—The Historical Background," *Environment International* 13 (1987): 19–25.
7. Both descriptions come from Rhys Richards, "The Maritime Fur Trade: Sealers and Other Residents on St. Paul and Amsterdam Islands," *The Great Circle* 6, nos. 1, 2 (1984):48ff.
8. Charles Darwin, *The Voyage of the Beagle,* edited by Leonard Engel (New York: Doubleday, 1962).
9. James Kirker, *Adventures to China: Americans in the Southern Oceans, 1792–1812* (New York: Oxford University Press, 1970).
10. Richard M. Laws, "The Ecology of the Southern Ocean," *American Scientist* 73 (January–February 1985): 26–40.

Chapter 2: Breaking the Ice

1. Jared Diamond, "Ten Thousand Years of Solitude," *Discover,* March 1993, pp. 48–58.

2. United States Coast Guard, "Welcome Aboard USCGC Polar Sea (WAGB-11)."
3. Arnold L. Gordon and Josefino C. Comiso, "Polynyas in the Southern Ocean," *Scientific American* 258, 6 (1988):90ff.
4. *Ibid.*
5. David L. Garrison, Cornelius W. Sullivan, and Stephen F. Ackley, "Sea Ice Microbial Communities in Antarctica," *Bioscience* 36, no. 4 (1986):243–50.

Chapter 3: Sealing

1. A. Grenfell Price, ed., *The Explorations of Captain James Cook in the Pacific: As Told by Selections of His Own Journals, 1768–1779* (New York: Dover Publications, 1971).
2. *Ibid.*, p. 148.
3. *Ibid.*, p. 7.
4. *Ibid.*, p. 7.
5. *Ibid.*, pp. 1–2.
6. *Ibid.*, p. 109.
7. *Ibid.*, p. 111.
8. *Ibid.*, p. 112.
9. *Ibid.*, p. 113.
10. *Ibid.*, pp. 146, 150.
11. *Ibid.*, p. 185.
12. *Ibid.*, p. 186.
13. *Ibid.*, p. 187.
14. The information on northern sealing is from W. Nigel Bonner, *Seals and Man* (Seattle: University of Washington Press, 1982). The description of sealing at Anholt comes from pp. 30–31.
15. *Ibid.*, p. 60. Bonner writes:

    It is strange to read again and again in sealers' accounts that the seals had abandoned the rocks. Clearly, what had happened in these cases was that the seals, remaining faithful to their now-insecure breeding grounds returned to be greeted with a sealer's club and death. Perhaps by their euphemism the sealers salved their consciences and kept alive the hope that they yet might find the rocks whither the seal herds had departed.

16. Thomas A. Stevens, "The First American Sealers in the Antarctic, 1812–1819 and The First Voyage of The Brig *Hersilia*, of Stonington, Conn., 1819–1820," prepared for U.S. Department of State, May 1, 1954.
17. Bonner, *Seals and Man*, p. 61.
18. Stevens, "The First American Sealers . . . "
19. Bonner, *Seals and Man*, p. 59.
20. James Kirker, *Adventures to China: Americans in the Southern Oceans, 1792–1812* (New York: Oxford University Press, 1970), p. 102. Kirker attributes this quotation to the diary of Ebenezer Townsend, Jr.
21. Kirker, *Adventures to China*. Quoted from *Voyages Round the World*, by Edmund Fanning, New York, 1833.
22. "Narrative of Sealing and Trading Voyage," University Microfilms, Ann Arbor, Michigan. Facsimile copy from Papers of the New Haven Historical Society, vol 5., New Haven, Connecticut, 1894, "Narrative of a Sealing and Trading Voyage, in the ship Huron, from New Haven, around the world, September 1802, to October 1806, By Joel Root, the Supercargo."
23. *Ibid.*
24. Bonner, *Seals and Man*, p. 62.
25. *Ibid.*
26. Kirker, *Adventures to China*.
27. Rhys Richards, "The Maritime Fur Trade: Sealers and Other Residents on St. Paul and Amsterdam Islands," *The Great Circle* 6, nos. 1, 2 (1984).
28. *Ibid.*
29. *Ibid.*
30. Edouard A. Stackpole, *The Voyage of the* Huron *and the* Huntress, (Mystic, Conn.: [n.p.], 1955).
31. Richards, "The Maritime Fur Trade."
32. Briton Cooper Busch, ed., *Master of Desolation: The Reminiscences of Whaling Captain Joseph J. Fuller* (Mystic, Conn.: Mystic Seaport Museum, 1980), pp. 20–21.
33. *Ibid.*, p. 117.
34. *Ibid.*, p. 168.
35. *Ibid.*, p. 170.

36. *Ibid.*, p. 184.
37. *Ibid.*, p. 280.
38. John Nunn, *Wreck of the Favorite*, edited by W. B. Clarke, M.D. (New York: Vintage Books/The Library of America, 1993). This is an account of Nunn's shipwreck on Desolation Island.
39. Apsley Cherry-Garrard, *The Worst Journey in the World: Antarctica 1910–1913* (New York: Carroll & Graf, 1989).

Chapter 4: Port

1. Roland Huntford, *Scott and Amundsen: The Race to the South Pole* (New York: Putnam, 1980).

Chapter 5: Larval Shapes

1. Nicholson Baker, in *U and I* (New York: Random House, 1991), his book-length essay on his obsession with Updike, writes of Updike's sexual metaphors: "Once the sensation of the interior of a vagina has been compared to a ballet slipper (if my memory doesn't distort that unlocatable simile) the sexual revolution is complete. . . ." [p. 18].
2. John Updike, "The Other," collected in *Trust Me* (New York: Fawcett Crest, 1987), p. 178.

Chapter 6: Higher Forms

1. Sanford Moss, *Natural History of the Antarctic Peninsula* (New York: Columbia University Press, 1988), p. 83.
2. *Ibid.*, p. 75.
3. Richard M. Laws, "The Ecology of the Southern Ocean," *American Scientist* 73 (January–February 1985):26–40.
4. Stephen Nicol and William de la Mare, "Ecosystem Management and the Antarctic Krill," *American Scientist* 81 (January–February 1985):36–47.
5. *Ibid.*, p. 41. Nicol and de la Mare point out that "The current catch of all species from all the world's oceans and seas is only 99 million tons."
6. Moss, *Natural History of the Antarctic Peninsula*, p. 69.
7. Rachel Carson, *The Sea Around Us* (New York: The Limited Editions Club, 1980), p. 25.

8. John Nunn, *Wreck of the Favorite,* edited by W. B. Clarke, M.D. (New York: Vintage Books/The Library of America, 1993).
9. Robert Cushman Murphy, *Oceanic Birds of South America* (New York: American Museum of Natural History, 1936).

    The sighting of an albatross the first time is also recounted in *Moby Dick* by Melville's narrator, Ishmael, and given an added sense of wonder and dread by the meditation on whiteness (such as that of the whale) to which it is a footnote. This albatross was not seen in flight:

    I remember the first albatross I ever saw. It was during a prolonged gale, in waters hard upon the Antarctic seas. From my forenoon watch below, I ascended to the overclouded deck; and there, dashed upon the main hatches, I saw a regal, feathery thing of unspotted whiteness, and with a hooked, Roman bill sublime. At intervals, it arched forth its vast archangel wings, as if to embrace some holy ark.

    After describing a mystical experience, "As Abraham before the angels I bowed myself etc. . . . ," Ishmael returns to the physical presence before him on deck.

    But how had the mystic thing been caught? Whisper it not, and I will tell; with a treacherous hook and line, as the fowl floated on the sea. At last the Captain made a postman of it; tying a lettered, leathern tally round its neck, with the ship's time and place; and letting it escape. But I doubt not, that leathern tally, meant for man, was taken off in Heaven, when the white fowl flew to joing the wing-folding, the invoking, and adoring cherubim!

10. R. B. Robertson, *Of Whales and Men* (New York: Alfred A. Knopf, 1954), p. 90.

Chapter 7: Whaling

1. F. D. Ommaney, *Lost Leviathan* (London: Hutchinson & Co., 1971), p. 84.

2. George Deacon, *The Antarctic Circumpolar Ocean* (Cambridge, England: Cambridge University Press, 1984), p. 55.
3. Robert Cushman Murphy, *Logbook for Grace* (New York: Macmillan, 1947), p. 141.
4. Ommaney, *Lost Leviathan*, p. 103.
5. *Ibid.*, pp. 101–2.
6. Murphy, *Logbook for Grace*, p. 143.
7. R. B. Robertson, *Of Whales and Men* (New York: Knopf, 1954), p. 58.
8. Ommaney, *Lost Leviathan*, p. 14.
9. Robertson, *Of Whales and Men*, p. 27.
10. Ommaney, *Lost Leviathan*, p. 145.
11. Robertson, *Of Whales and Men*, p. 125.
12. Ommaney, *Lost Leviathan*, pp. 38–39. Ommaney writes:

> There were always long faces at South Georgia when the Sei whales appeared in February for it was taken to mean that no more of the bigger Rorquals would be caught that season, or fewer anyway. This was usually true because they had by then passed the island on their way southward and the Seis were believed to be following in their wake from the coast of South America.

13. Deacon, *The Antarctic Circumpolar Ocean*, p. 61.
14. *Ibid.*, p. 65.
15. Ommaney, *Lost Leviathan*, p. 11.
16. *Ibid.*, p. 15.
17. Robertson, *Of Whales and Men*, p. 158.
18. Michael D. Lemonick, "The hunt, the furor," *Time Magazine*, August 2, 1993, p. 42.
19. John Darnton, "Norweigians Claim Their Whaling Rights," *New York Times*, August 7, 1993.
20. Gary Snyder, "Mother Earth: Her Whales," in *We Animals*, edited by Nadya Eisenberg (San Francisco: Sierra Club Books, 1989), pp. 71–73.
21. Karel Čapek, *The War with the Newts*, translated by Ewald Osers (Highland Park, N.J.: Catbird Press, 1990).
22. "Whaling Around Antarctica Is Banned by World Body," *New York Times*, May 27, 1994, p. A2.

Chapter 9: The Ocean

1. Jonathan Raban, ed., *The Oxford Book of the Sea* (New York: Oxford University Press, 1992).
2. Alan Villiers, *The War Against Cape Horn* (New York: Charles Scribner's Sons, 1971).
3. *Ibid.*, p. 100.
4. *Ibid.*, pp. 41–42.
5. William Albert Robinson, *To the Great Southern Sea* (London: Peter Davies, 1966).
6. *Ibid.*, p. 73
7. George Deacon, *The Antarctic Circumpolar Ocean* (Cambridge, England: Cambridge University Press, 1984), p. 140.
8. Rachel Carson, *The Sea Around Us* (New York: The Limited Editions Club, 1980), p. 128.
9. Deacon, *The Antarctic Circumpolar Ocean,* p. 141.
10. Robinson, *To the Great Southern Sea,* p. 76.

Appendix

A NOTE ON SOURCES

In writing this book I relied not only on interviews and personal experience, but on a number of written sources. Those from which I drew specific information are cited in the chapter notes. Some books were particularly helpful, however, in inspiring me and in providing information on subjects in which I had no firsthand experience.

First and foremost was a small volume by George Deacon, *The Antarctic Circumpolar Ocean*, a brief overview of the ocean in all its aspects, and the only such book that I know of. The book was invaluable in giving me a basic grounding in information about the Southern Ocean, and also inspired me to try to do a book of more general interest on an ocean that has not gotten the attention that the Antarctic continent has. In a more literary sense I was inspired by *A Logbook for Grace*, by Robert Cushman Murphy, whose knowledge of this world and skill in describing it remains unsurpassed.

On Nature, a collection of essays about the natural world, edited by Daniel Halpern, is full of wonderful reflections on the natural world and on writing about the natural world. Of all the reading I did, this collection most stimulated me to think about how we imagine the world around us. Also very helpful was *Man and the Natural World: A History of the Modern Sensibility,* by Keith Thomas.

I'm afraid there are few original thoughts in my work. Even the ones that struck me as my own were no doubt lifted from philsophers or poets or historians I encountered along the way. Two other books that I did not draw on specifically, but which served in different ways as models of writing about cold places were *South Light,* by Michael Parfit, and Barry Lopez's *Arctic Dreams,* the first for its narrative flow, humor, and eye for human behavior, and the latter for its depth, passion, and force.

Other books of importance for the history and science they cover, all of which are listed in the Notes, are: *Seals and Men,* by W. Nigel Bonner; *Lost Leviathan,* by F. D. Ommaney; *Of Whales and Men,* by R. B. Robertson; and *Natural History of the Antarctic Peninsula,* by Sanford Moss.

And finally, the shortest book of all is my favorite in the writing about Antarctica and its surrounding waters: *Shackleton's Boat Journey.* The reasons are several: On my first trip south I traveled the same path, from Elephant Island to South Georgia, that Shackleton did. Of the places I've traveled to, South Georgia is the one that has affected me most strongly. And F. A. Worsley, in his matter-of-fact, unwriterly way, tells his story so well that I take the book as an important lesson, and one I hope someday to learn.

INDEX

Aborigines, Tasmanian, 17–18
Acoustic imaging, 152–54
Acronyms used at McMurdo Research Station, 83–84
"Adam's Task" (Hollander), 4
Adelie penguins, 48, 49, 85, 118
"Against Nature" (Oates), 2, 102
Agassiz, Louis, 112
Albatrosses, 25, 57, 72, 114–16, 121–22
Algae, 38–39, 109
"Aloft con" of *Polar Sea,* 22, 44
Amphipods, 90
Amsterdam Island, 12, 66
Amundsen, Roald, 1, 19–20, 76–77, 89
Anasterias rupicola, 110
Anchor ice, 90
Anholt Island, 60
Anson, George, 159–60
Antarctica (ship), 128
Antarctica
  climate of, 81
  diving in, 84–87, 89
  first trip to, 2–3, 5–7, 13
Antarctic Circle, 43, 45, 55, 57
Antarctic Circumpolar Ocean, 7–8. *See also* Southern Ocean
Antarctic Circumpolar Ocean (Deacon), 179
Antarctic Convergence, 7, 120
Antarctic Ocean. *See* Southern Ocean
Antarctic Program, New Zealand, 76, 89, 103
Antarctic Program, U.S., 14
Antarctic Treaty, 88
Arctic Dreams (Lopez), 180
Arctic Ocean, 7
  ice cover of, 33–34
Arroyo, Jorge, 42, 150–51
Aspasia (ship), 64
Astronomy, 169
Atmospheric conditions, 33–35
Australia, 8

Bahia Paraiso (ship), 47
Baleen whales, 13, 127–28, 129, 134–35
Balleny, John, 40

Balleny Islands, 40
Basch, Larry, 86, 87, 89, 93–94, 96–97
Beardmore Glacier, 79
Beckett, Samuel, 157
Berg, Jonathan, 20–21, 41, 48
Betsey (ship), 64
B-6 iceberg, 168
Bird Island, 121–22
Bird life, 9, 10, 114–20. *See also* Penguins
  albatrosses, 25, 57, 72, 114–16, 121–22
  petrels, 27, 39, 47, 116–17, 153
  pipit, 121
  sheath bill, 117
  skuas, 48–50, 87, 117
Birdwatching, 4–6
  fanaticism of birdwatchers, 5–6
Bligh, William, 9, 12
Blubber boys, 134
Blue whales, 134–35
Borchgrevink, Carsten, 112
Bouvet island, 54
Bowers, H. R. "Birdie," 119
Boyer, Gary, 25
Brine channels, 38, 39
British Admiralty Research Laboratory, 162

Camp Evans, 77
Cape Horn, 3, 54, 159–61, 162
Čapek, Karel, 140
Cape petrels, 39
Capilene underwear, 86
Carbon, 147
Carson, Rachel, 114, 162
Channichthyidae, 111–12
Chanticleer, H.M.S. (ship), 65
Chaplin, Charlie, 126
Cherry-Garrard, Apsley, 74, 118–19
China, sealing and, 62, 63, 65
Circumpolar current, 8, 9
Civilian workers in Antarctica, 78
Clarke, Arthur C., 96
Climate changes, 33–35
Clothing. *See* Gear
Coast Guard, 14, 21, 26, 36, 47, 87, 99, 145, 146, 167. *See also* Polar Sea
Coleridge, Samuel, 10, 115
Colonizing of Tasmania, 17–18
Congelation ice, 36–37
Continent, transition from sea to shore, 10
Continental drift, 8
Cook, James, 7, 9, 11, 12, 55–58, 64, 134, 161
  biography of, 55
  discovery of South Georgia, 58, 59, 64
Crab eater seals, 68
Crean, Tom, 122–23
Crew of *Polar Sea,* 20–21, 22, 35–36, 42, 43, 44, 145, 150–51, 156, 157, 158, 164
Cross polarization, 101
Crozet Islands, 61
Cuisine. *See* Food

Currents, ocean, 9, 34, 144
Cushman Murphy, Robert. *See* Murphy, Robert Cushman

Da Gama, Vasco, 11
Daisy (ship), 129
Dana, James D., 113
Darwin, Charles, 12
Davis, John, 68
Deacon, George, 135, 162, 179
Deception Island, 128
Desolation Island. *See* Kerguelen
Dias, Bartholomeu, 11
Diatoms, 38, 109, 147
Diaz de Solfs, Juan, 60
Discovery (ship), 76, 162
Discovery Committee, 135–36
Diseases, 55–56
Diving, 84–87, 89
  gear for, 86–87
Dragon fish, 112
Drake, Francis, 53–54
Drake Passage, 8, 54, 160
Drills, 81
  aboard *Polar Sea*, 21–22, 23
Drygalski Ice Tongue, 104
Dry suits, 86
Dry valleys of Transantarctic Mountains, 105–8
Dunbar, Rob, 145
D'Urville, Dumont, 161
DVs (distinguished visitors), 83

Edes, Samuel B., 66–67
Eggs of fish, 111
Elephant seals, 68–71, 72–73, 121
  killing of, 69–71
Emperor penguins, 74, 119
Empress (ship), 13
Endeavor (ship), 122
End of Nature, The (McKibben), 95–96
Environmental Defense Fund, 89
Environmental issues, 87–89, 90, 137–38. *See also* Greenpeace
  fuel leaks, 41–44, 46–47, 47–48
  waste management, 87–88, 90, 91, 95, 96, 107–8
Equipment. *See* Gear
Eskimos, 59
Euphausia superba, 113
Evans, Edgar, 112

Fairbanks, Alaska, 35
Fanning, Edmund, 61–64, 67
Filchner-Ronne Shelf, 11
Fin whales, 135
Fish and fishing, 109, 110–12
Fog, 24–25, 28, 39, 40
Food
  aboard *Polar Sea*, 20, 23–24, 36, 168
  aboard *World Discoverer*, 3
  on Captain Cook's explorations, 56
Foyn, Svend, 127
Franklin Island, 48, 164
Frazil ice, 37

Free Willy (film), 137
Fuel leaks, 41–44, 46–47, 47–48
Fuller, Joseph, 70–72, 127
Fur seals, 59, 60–61, 68, 121
  killing of, 67

Gas chromatography, 151
Gear, 19–20, 21
  for diving, 86–87
GFAs (general field assistants), 83
Giant petrels, 117
Glaciers, 10, 79, 102, 104
Glaciology, 35–38
Global warming, 33–34
Golden Eagle (clipper ship), 160
Gondwana (Greenpeace ship), 50, 90
Gondwanaland, 8
Gordon, Arnold, 35, 143
Granite Harbor, 149
Granular ice, 37
Gray, Spalding, 101, 102
Grease ice, 37
Great-winged petrel, 117
Greenpeace, 50, 77, 83, 87–90
Green Wave (cargo ship), 99
Grytviken, 136

Hair seals, 62–63
Halley, Edmund, 54
Halpern, Daniel, 179–80
Hammer, William, 79
Hardin, Garrett, 61
Harpoon gun, 127, 128, 132
Hatch, Joseph, 71
Hawaii, 58–59
Hawes, Ralph, 29
Hawkins, Richard, 56
Helicopters, 22, 28–29, 41, 47, 48, 87, 90, 103, 105, 107
Hemoglobin of ice fish, 111
Herpolsheimer, Jim, 84–85, 86, 89
Hobart, Tasmania, 17, 18
Hollander, John, 4
Holmes, Oliver Wendell, 25
Hopedale, Labrador, 35
Hotel California, at McMurdo Research Station, 77, 78–79, 102
Human waste, 87–88, 90, 91, 107–8
Humboldt Current, 144
Humpbacks, 135
Huntford, Roland, 77
Huron (ship), 63, 68
Hut Point, 76

Ice
  pack, 10, 36, 40, 168
  sea, 11, 34–35, 36–39
Icebergs, 3, 10, 29, 168
Ice birds. *See* Snow petrels
Icebreaking, 14, 15, 19, 28, 29–31, 39, 50–51, 75. *See also* Polar Sea
Ice caps, 9
Ice cover, 85
  of Arctic Ocean, 33–34
  of Southern Ocean, 10–11
Ice diving, 84–87, 89
  gear for, 86–87
Ice fish, 111–12

Ice shelves, 10, 11. *See also* Ross Ice Shelf
Ice slices, 101
Insects, 120
International Whaling Commission, 134, 139, 141
Invertebrates, 90, 93–94, 96–98, 109, 110

James Caird (ship), 122
Jeffries, Martin, 35–37, 41, 99, 101, 163, 169
Joseph Conrad (ship), 160
Juan Fernandez Islands, 64

Kerguelen, 12, 54, 71, 110, 127
Killer whales, 134, 137
King penguins, 121
Kraus, Scott, 138
Krill, 39, 111, 112–13

Lake Bonney, 105–8
Lamont Doherty Earth Observatory, 143
Larsen, C. A., 128, 130
Le Maire, Isaac, 54
Leopard seals, 68, 85–86
Lettau, Bernard, 47
Lewis, Sinclair, 126
Logbook for Grace (Murphy), 129, 179
Lopez, Barry, 180

Macaroni penguins, 118, 120
McKibben, Bill, 95–96
McMurdo Research Station, 14, 23, 35, 50, 51, 75–91, 163
  biology building at, 93–95
  environmental issues at, 87–89, 90
  Hotel California at, 77, 78–79, 102
  officers' club at, 99–100
McMurdo Sound, 76, 88–89, 90–91, 139
Macquarie Island, 71
Magellan, Ferdinand, 11, 53
Manahan, Donal, 97–98, 105
Marine biology, 93
Marine life, 9–10, 38–39, 93–94, 96–97. *See also* Microscopic life; *and specific animals*
  environmental issues concerning, 90–91
  fish, 109, 110–12
  invertebrates, 90, 93–94, 96–98, 109, 110
  krill, 39, 111, 112–13
  starfish, 94, 96–98, 110
Meals. *See* Food
Melville, Herman, 60
Microscopic life, 38–39, 106
  algae, 38–39, 109
  diatoms, 38, 109, 147
  nematodes, 107
  phytoplankton, 107
Microtone tool, 101
Military life, 77, 80–81, 145, 146–47
Minke whales, 6, 99, 138, 139–40
Mission definition, 146–47
Modern Times (film), 126

Moorings for sediment traps, 147–52, 155, 157–58
Moser, Chris, 145, 146, 148
Moss, Sanford, 7, 110
Moss Landing Marine Laboratories, 90
"Mother Earth: Her Whales" (Snyder), 140
Mucciarone, Dave, 145, 146, 149–50, 155, 157–58
Murphy, Robert Cushman, 114–15, 116, 129, 130, 137, 179

Nathaniel B. Palmer (ship), 68
National Science Foundation (NSF), 14, 19, 47, 68, 79, 83, 88–89, 90, 100, 167
Nematodes, 107
New Zealand Antarctic Program, 76, 89, 103
NGA (nongovernmental activity), 83, 88
Northern Ellsmere Island, 35
Nototheniiformes, 110
NSF (National Science Foundation). *See* National Science Foundation

Oates, Joyce Carol, 2, 102
Oceanography, 143–58
Oceans. *See also* Arctic Ocean; Southern Ocean
  circulation of, 10
  currents of, 9, 34, 144
  quotes about, 25–26
  salinity of, 10, 41
  understanding, 4–5
Ocean swell, 25, 165
Ochs, Phil, 80
O'Keeffe, Georgia, 97
Oliver, John, 90–91
Ommaney, F. D., 129–30, 132, 137
On Nature (Halpern, ed.), 179–80
Orcas, 134, 137

Pacific Islanders, 12
Pack ice, 10, 36, 40, 168. *See also* Sea ice
Pagothenia borchgrevinki, 112
Palmer, Nathaniel B., 68
Palmer Land, 68
Palmer Station, fuel leak near, 47–48
Paramour (ship), 54
Parfit, Michael, 180
Pembroke (ship), 55
Penguins, 9, 11, 57, 117–20, 121
  Adelie, 48, 49, 85, 118
  emperor, 74, 119
  harvesting of, 71
  king, 121
  Macaroni, 118, 120
  watching for, 2–3
Petrels, 27, 39, 47, 116–17, 153
Phelps, William, 67, 69–70
Phytoplankton, 107
Pickering (ship), 66–67
Pierson, Geoff, 152, 153
Pintados, 39

Pipits, 121
Planktivory, 110
Platelet ice, 37–38
Plunder fish, 112
Pogronphryne scotti, 112
Polar Sea (Coast Guard cutter), 15, 99
  crew of, 20–21, 22, 35–36, 42, 43, 44, 145, 150–51, 156, 157, 158, 164
  drills aboard, 21–22, 23
  first ice sighted by, 27
  fuel leak of, 41–44, 46–47
  icebreaking of, 28, 29–31, 39, 50–51, 75
  initiation ceremony of new sailors, 45–46
  meals aboard, 20, 23–24, 36, 168
  physical description of, 18–19, 21, 22, 43–44, 46
  research cruise of, 139, 144–58
  return voyage of, 162–70
Polynyas, 34–35, 143
Price, A. Grenfell, 56
Prionadraco evansi, 112
Professor Zubov (ship), 99–100

Ramapo, U.S.S. (ship), 162
Recycling, 90. *See also* Environmental issues
Reeves Glacier, 102
Reindeer, 122
Resolution (ship), 55, 134
Respiratory system of ice fish, 111–12
"Rime of the Ancient Mariner, The" (Coleridge), 10, 115
Robertson, R. B., 131–33, 137
Robinson, W. A., 161, 162, 163
Roll of vessel, 19, 21, 157, 165–66
Root, Joel, 63
Rorquals, 13, 127–28, 129, 134–35
Ross, James, 38, 111
Ross Ice Shelf, 11, 76, 102, 112, 149, 166
Ross Island, 75. *See also* McMurdo Research Station
Ross Sea, 50, 139
  research cruise around, 139, 144–58
Ross seals, 68

Sabrina Island, 47
St. Paul Island, 12, 66
Salinity of ocean, 10, 41
Salisbury Plain, 121
Scale worm, 94
Schouten, Willem, 54
Schrödinger's Swell, 21
Schultz, Bill, 27
Schwarzenegger movies, aboard *Polar Sea*, 24, 145
Scientific research, 143–58
  nature of, 98, 152–53
Scoresby, William, 161–62
Scott, Robert Falcon, 20, 76–77, 102, 112, 118–19
Scott Island, 165

Scott's hut, 86, 89, 103
Scott's Hut Race, 76
Scurvy, 55–56
Sea Around Us, The (Carson), 114, 162
Sea ice, 11, 34–35. *See also* Pack ice
  kinds of, 36–38
  microscopic life living in, 38–39
Sealing, 12–13, 59–74, 126
  early history of, 59–62
  economy of, 62, 63–64, 73
  killing methods, 67, 69–71, 73
  regulation of, 65
Sea lions, 62–63
Seals, 9, 10, 12–13
  crab eater, 68
  elephant, 68–71, 72–73, 121
  fur, 59, 60–61, 67, 68, 121
  hair, 62–63
  leopard, 68, 85–86
  Ross seals, 68
  sea lions, 62–63
  Weddell, 68, 85
Sea stars, 94, 96–98, 110
Sediment traps, 145, 146–52, 157
Sei whales, 135
Selkirk, Alexander, 64
Shackleton, Ernest, 9, 76, 77, 122–24, 180
Shackleton's Boat Journey (Worsley), 180
Shaw, Sef, 164
Sheath bill, 117
Shelters, snow, 81–83
Siebrands, Alda, 22
Signy Island, 116
Silica, 147
Skuas, 48–50, 87, 117
Smith, William, 65
Snow petrels, 27, 39, 57, 153
Snow school, at McMurdo Research Station, 80–83
Snow shelters, 81–83
Snyder, Gary, 140
South Africa, 60
South America, 8, 54, 65
Southern Cross, 169
Southern Ocean
  boundaries of, 8
  early explorations of, 11–12, 53–59
  ecosystem of, 9–10, 11, 109–24
  as a global heat sink, 34
  ice covers, 10–11
  islands of, 12–13
  natural history of, 8–9
  oceanography and, 143–58
  sealing in, 12–13, 59–74, 126
  size and nature of waves in, 161–62
  whaling in, 13, 60, 123, 125–41
South Georgia, 9, 12, 120–23
  discovery by Cook, 58, 59, 64
  fishing rights off, 110
  whaling factories on, 127, 129–30, 131, 136

South Light (Parfit), 180
South Orkneys, 116, 117
South Pole, 1, 76–77, 83
South Shetland Islands, 65, 67, 128
Sperm whales, 60, 126–27, 129, 134
Stackpole, Edouard, 68
Starfish, 94, 96–98, 110
Stearns, Chuck, 100, 102, 103–4, 165
Stevens, Wallace, 2
Storm petrels, 47, 116–17
Strom Ness Camp, 123–24
Strom Ness Harbor, 122
Superb euphausid, 113
Swedish South Polar Expedition, 128
Swell, ocean, 25, 165

Tahitians, 56
Tasmania, 17–18
Tasmanian aborigines, 17–18
Taylor Valley, 105–6
Terra Nova Bay, 49
Thomas, Keith, 180
Thompson, Dale, 20–21
Thule, Greenland, 35
Tourism, 167
Transantarctic Mountains, 50, 105–8, 158
Trillin, Calvin, 28
Twin Otter ski plane, 102, 103–4

U-barrels, 83
United States Exploring Expedition, 112, 113
Updike, John, 96, 101–2
Uruguay, 60, 65

Valparaiso, Chile, 163
Van Allard, Gary, 156, 157, 158
Ventifacts, 105, 108
Victoria Land, 49
Villiers, Allan, 160–61
Vostok, 100
Voyage Around the World, A (Anson), 159–60

War with the Newts, The (Čapek), 140
Waste management, 87–88, 90, 91, 95, 96, 107–8
Waves, 161–62, 165
Weather stations, 102, 104
Weddell, James, 64, 65
Weddell Sea, 34, 128
Weddell seals, 68, 85
Weeks, Willie, 35–37, 41, 101, 163
Welborn, John, 100, 105, 107, 108
West Wind Drift (circumpolar current), 8, 9
Whales, 10, 13, 57, 99
  baleen, 13, 127–28, 129, 134–35
  blue, 134–35
  humpbacks, 135
  killer, 134, 137
  minke, 6, 99, 138, 139–40
  sperm, 60, 126–27, 129, 134
Whale watching, 6–7, 138, 139–40

Whaling, 13, 60, 123, 125–41
factories on South Georgia, 127, 129–30, 131, 136
factory ships for, 128, 131–34, 136
harpoon gun, use of, 127, 128, 132
products produced, 126–27, 133–34, 138
regulation of, 134, 139, 141
Whitbread 'Round the World Race, 161, 166
Wilkes, Charles, 112, 113
Willy Field, 103
Wilson, Edward, 76
Wilson, William, 116–17, 119
Wind speed, 164–65
Wines, aboard *Polar Sea*, 20
Winter Quarters Bay, 90
Woodall, James, 56
World Discoverer (cruise ship), 2–3, 5–7, 13
Worsley, Frank A., 122–23, 180
Worst Journey in the World, The (Cherry-Garrard), 74, 118–19

Young Island, 40